Withdrawn

MAGELLAN
Over the Edge of the World

THE TRUE STORY OF THE TERRIFYING
FIRST CIRCUMNAVIGATION OF THE GLOBE

LAURENCE BERGREEN

ROARING BROOK PRESS   New York

Published by Roaring Brook Press
Roaring Brook Press is a division of Holtzbrinck Publishing Holdings Limited Partnership
175 Fifth Avenue, New York, New York 10010
mackids.com

Adapted from *Over the Edge of the World: Magellan's Terrifying Circumnavigation of the Globe* by
Laurence Bergreen, published in 2003 by William Morrow, an imprint of HarperCollins.

Library of Congress Cataloging-in-Publication Data
Names: Bergreen, Laurence.
Title: Magellan : over the edge of the world / Laurence Bergreen.
Description: New York : Roaring Brook Press, 2016. | Children's adaptation of author's
work entitled: Over the edge of the world.
Identifiers: LCCN 2015035814 | ISBN 9781626721203 (hardback) | ISBN
9781626721210 (ebook)
Subjects: LCSH: Magalhäaes, Fernäao de, 1521—Juvenile literature. | Explorers—
Portugal—Biography—Juvenile literature. | Voyages around the world—History—
16th century—Juvenile literature. | BISAC: JUVENILE NONFICTION / History /
Exploration & Discovery. | JUVENILE NONFICTION / History / Europe. |
JUVENILE NONFICTION / Transportation / Boats, Ships & Underwater Craft.
Classification: LCC G286.M2 B55 2016 | DDC 910.4/1—dc23
LC record available at http://lccn.loc.gov/2015035814

Our books may be purchased in bulk for promotional, educational, or business use. Please contact
your local bookseller or the Macmillan Corporate and Premium Sales Department at (800) 221-7945
ext. 5442 or by e-mail at MacmillanSpecialMarkets@macmillan.com.

First edition, 2017
Book design by Elliot Kreloff
Maps by Cathy Bobak
Printed in the United States of America by LSC Communications,
Harrisonburg, Virginia

1   3   5   7   9   10   8   6   4   2

To Zata Brielle Fray

CONTENTS

MAJOR CHARACTERS

Juan de Aranda (merchant)

Beatriz Barbosa (Magellan's wife)

Diogo Barbosa (Magellan's father-in-law)

Charles I (king of Spain)

Ruy Faleiro (cosmographer)

Manuel I (king of Portugal)

Juan Rodríguez de Fonseca (bishop of Burgos, later archbishop)

THE ARMADA DE MOLUCCA

(listed according to positions at the outset of the circumnavigation)

Trinidad

FERDINAND MAGELLAN (captain general)

Francisco Albo (pilot)

Duarte Barbosa (Magellan's brother-in-law)

Enrique (Magellan's slave, also an interpreter)

Gonzalo Gómez de Espinosa (*alguacil*, or master-at-arms)

Estêvão Gomes (pilot)

Ginés de Mafra (pilot)

Martín Méndez (purser)

Álvaro de Mesquita (Magellan's cousin)

Antonio Pigafetta (chronicler)

Cristóvão Rebêlo (Magellan's illegitimate son)

Pedro de Valderrama (chaplain)

San Antonio

JUAN DE CARTAGENA (captain and inspector general)
Antonio de Coca (fleet accountant)
Gerónimo Guerra (clerk)
Diego Hernández (mate)
Juan de Lorriage (master)
Pero Sánchez de la Reina (priest)
Andrés de San Martín (cosmographer and astronomer)

Concepción

GASPAR DE QUESADA (captain)
Hernando de Bustamante (barber)
João Lopes Carvalho (pilot)
Joãozito Carvalho (cabin boy)
Juan Sebastián Elcano (master)
Luis de Molino (servant)

Victoria

LUIS DE MENDOZA (captain)

Santiago

JUAN RODRÍGUEZ SERRANO (captain)

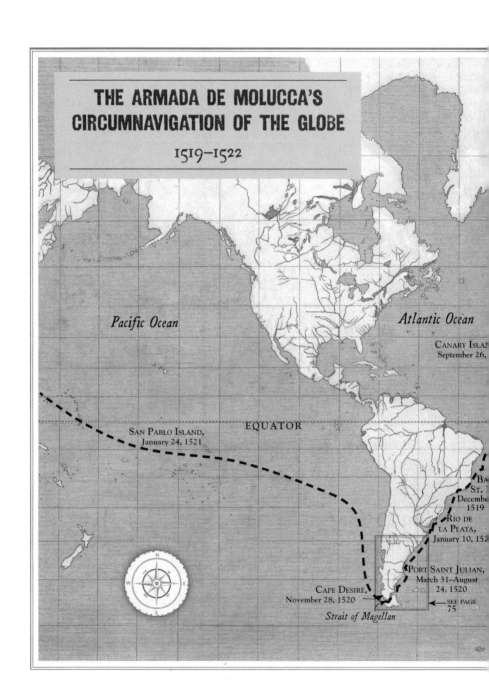

THE ARMADA DE MOLUCCA'S CIRCUMNAVIGATION OF THE GLOBE

1519–1522

Pacific Ocean

Atlantic Ocean

CANARY ISLAN
September 26,

Pacific Ocean

SAN PABLO ISLAND,
January 24, 1521

EQUATOR

BA
ST.
Decembe
1519

RIO DE
LA PLATA,
January 10, 152

PORT SAINT JULIAN,
March 31–August
24, 1520

CAPE DESIRE,
November 28, 1520

SEE PAGE
75

Strait of Magellan

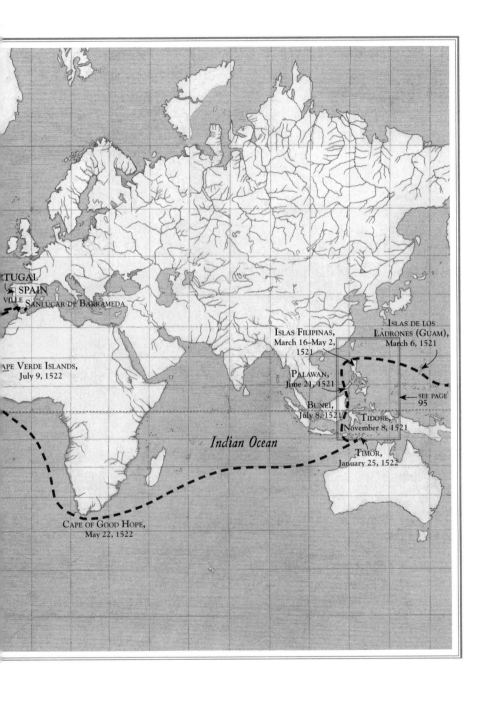

RTUGAL

SPAIN

VILLE SANLÚCAR DE BARRAMEDA

CAPE VERDE ISLANDS,
July 9, 1522

ISLAS FILIPINAS,
March 16–May 2,
1521

ISLAS DE LOS
LADRONES (GUAM),
March 6, 1521

PALAWAN,
June 21, 1521

BUNEI,
July 8, 1521

TIDORE,
November 8, 1521

SEE PAGE
95

Indian Ocean

TIMOR,
January 25, 1522

CAPE OF GOOD HOPE,
May 22, 1522

A Note on Dates

Dates are given in the Julian calendar, in use in Europe at the time of Magellan's voyage. In 1582, sixty years after the completion of Magellan's voyage, Spain, France, and other European countries migrated to the Gregorian calendar, decreed by Pope Gregory XIII and designed to correct flaws in the Julian system. Ten days were omitted, so that October 5, 1582, in the Julian calendar suddenly became October 15, 1582, in the Gregorian.

Magellan's voyage had its own record-keeping issues. The dates of various events recorded by the two chief chroniclers of the expedition, Antonio Pigafetta and Francisco Albo, occasionally diverge by one day. Albo, a pilot, followed the custom of ships' logs, which began the day at noon rather than at midnight. In contrast, Pigafetta used a non-nautical frame of reference in his diary. So an event occurring on a given morning might have been put down a day apart in the records maintained by the two.

Finally, the international date line, demarcating one calendar day from the next, did not exist at the time of Magellan's voyage. (It now extends from the North Pole to the South Pole, through the Pacific Ocean.) As Albo and Pigafetta neared the completion of their circumnavigation, they were astonished to note that their calculations were off and that their voyage around the world had taken one day longer than they had thought.

PROLOGUE
A GHOSTLY APPARITION

On September 6, 1522, a battered ship appeared on the horizon near the port of Sanlúcar de Barrameda, Spain.

As the ship drew closer, people gathered onshore noticed that her tattered sails flailed in the breeze, that her rigging had rotted away, that the sun had bleached her colors, and that storms had damaged her sides. A small pilot boat was dispatched to lead the strange ship over the reefs to the harbor. Those aboard the pilot boat found themselves looking into the face of every sailor's nightmare. The vessel they were guiding into the harbor was manned by a skeleton crew of just eighteen malnourished souls suffering from scurvy; most lacked the strength to walk or even to speak. Their tongues were swollen, and their bodies were covered with painful boils. Their captain was dead, as were the officers and the pilots.

Three years earlier, their ship, *Victoria,* had belonged to a fleet of five vessels manned by 260 sailors under the command of Ferdinand Magellan, a Portuguese navigator sailing for Spain, with a charter to explore parts of the world unknown to Europeans and claim them for the Spanish crown. The expedition was one of the largest and best equipped ever mounted in the Age of Discovery, the period from around the 1400s to the 1700s, when Europeans began exploring the world by sea. Now *Victoria* and her ravaged little crew was all that was left, a ghost ship haunted by the memory of the fleet's lost sailors. Most had died excruciating deaths, some from scurvy, others by torture, and a few by drowning. Most shocking of all, Ferdinand Magellan himself had been murdered. Despite her brave name, *Victoria* was not a ship of triumph; she was a ship of agony.

But what a story the survivors had to tell: a chronicle of the most ambitious of all maritime expeditions; a tale of mutiny, of carousing on distant shores, and of exploring the entire globe; a story that changed the course of history and the way people saw the world. These survivors were the first to circumnavigate the entire earth. In the Age of Discovery, many voyages ended in disaster and were quickly forgotten, yet this one, despite the misfortunes that befell it, became the most important maritime expedition ever undertaken. The voyage demonstrated, among other things, that the earth was round, that the Americas were a separate continent (the New World), and that people lived everywhere on the planet. But the cost of these discoveries in terms of suffering and loss of life was greater than anyone could have anticipated. Had its captain, Fernão de Magalhães, whom we call Ferdinand Magellan, conquered the world, or is it more accurate to say the world conquered him?

CHAPTER ONE

THE QUEST

On June 7, 1494, Pope Alexander VI divided the world in half. The Treaty of Tordesillas established an imaginary line running down the middle of the Atlantic Ocean. Everything to the west of the line belonged to Spain, and everything to the east went to Spain's chief rival, Portugal. The only exception was Brazil, which Portugal also ruled.

Rather than settling the heated dispute over the New World, recently discovered by Christopher Columbus, the treaty ignited a furious race among nations to claim new lands and control the world's trade routes. At the time, Europeans were deeply ignorant of the world at large. Under the influence of Ptolemy—Claudius Ptolemaeus, a Greco-Egyptian mathematician and astronomer who lived in the second century CE—astronomers believed that the sun circled the earth. Ptolemy's influential work *Geography* spoke of a magnetic island; if ships sailed too close to it, the nails would be pulled from their hulls and the vessels would sink. Cartography (mapmaking) was often a matter of guesswork. The maps of 1494 depicted a world seamlessly combining heaven and earth. Mixing geography with mythology, adding phantom continents while neglecting real ones, cartographers made images of a world that never was. In the Age of Discovery, more than half the world was unexplored, unmapped, and misunderstood by Europeans. Although men of science and learning agreed that the earth was round, some mariners feared they could literally sail over the edge of the world.

Although enormous regions of the globe, previously blank, were getting filled in as explorers brought home news of their discoveries, especially in Africa, the true extent of the Pacific Ocean remained unknown. Even with this profound lack of understanding, Spain and Portugal competed to establish their global empires.

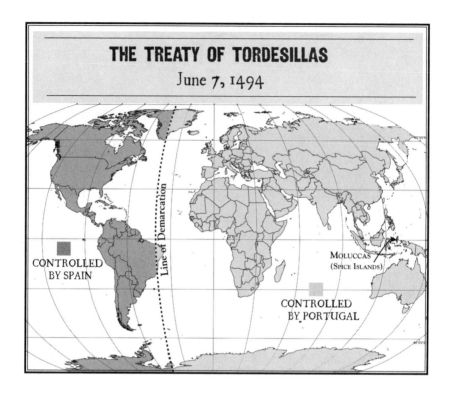

THE TREATY OF TORDESILLAS
June 7, 1494

Line of Demarcation

CONTROLLED BY SPAIN

MOLUCCAS (SPICE ISLANDS)

CONTROLLED BY PORTUGAL

Both the Spanish and the Portuguese recognized that a water route to the Indies—the area now known as India and Southeast Asia—could provide priceless merchandise, including the most precious commodity of all: spices.

Spices had played an essential economic role in civilizations since antiquity. In the Age of Discovery, the European quest for spices, like the global quest for oil today, drove the world's economy and influenced its politics; trade in spices became completely intertwined with exploration, conquest, and imperialism. But spices—white and black pepper, myrrh, frankincense, nutmeg, cinnamon, cassia, mace, and cloves, to name a few—evoked a glamour and aura all their own; for Europeans, the mere mention of their names summoned the wonders of the Orient and the mysterious East.

Arab merchants traded in spices via land routes reaching across Asia and became skilled at boosting prices by concealing the origins of their goods. The merchants maintained a virtual monopoly by insisting their precious wares came from Africa, when in fact they grew in various places in India, in China, and especially throughout Southeast Asia. Europeans came to believe that spices came from Africa, when in fact they only changed hands there.

Under the traditional system, spices, along with diamonds, pearls, opiates, and other goods from Asia, reached Europe by slow, costly, and indirect routes over land and sea, across China and the Indian Ocean, through the Middle East and the Persian Gulf. Merchants received them in Europe, usually in Italy or the South of France, and shipped them overland again to their final destination. Along the way, spices were sold as many as twelve different times, and every time they changed hands, their prices shot up.

Spices were the ultimate cash crop.

The global spice trade underwent an upheaval in 1453, when the great city of Constantinople (now Istanbul) fell to the Turks and the time-honored spice routes between Asia and Europe were severed. The prospect of establishing a spice trade via an ocean route, instead of the former overland routes, opened up new economic possibilities for any European nation able to master the seas. For those willing to assume the risks, the rewards of an oceanic spice trade, and the potential for control over the world's economy, were irresistible.

———————

Portugal was the first European nation to exploit the sea in its quest for spices and the global empire that went along with them. In the fifteenth and early sixteenth centuries, daring, even reckless mariners presented themselves to the Portuguese king to seek backing for their journeys of exploration. Among the most persistent supplicants was a minor nobleman with a long and checkered history in the service of the Portuguese empire in Africa: Fernão de Magalhães, or Ferdinand Magellan.

According to most accounts, Magellan was born in 1480, in the remote mountain village of Sabrosa, the seat of the family homestead. He spent his childhood in northwestern Portugal, within sight of the pounding surf of the Atlantic. His father, Rodrigo de Magalhães, traced his lineage back to an eleventh-century French crusader, De Magalhãis, who was given a grant of land by the Duke of Burgundy. Rodrigo himself qualified as minor Portuguese nobility and was remembered as a sheriff of the port of Aveiro.

Less is known about Magellan's mother, Alda de Mesquita, although there is room for intriguing speculation. The name *Mesquita*, meaning "mosque," was a common name among Portuguese *conversos*, converts from Judaism who sought to disguise their Jewish origins. It is possible that she had Jewish ancestry, and if she did, Ferdinand was also Jewish, according to custom. Nevertheless, the family considered itself Christian, and Ferdinand Magellan never thought of himself as anything other than a devout Catholic.

————

At twelve years of age, Ferdinand Magellan moved with his brother, Diogo, to the Portuguese capital, Lisbon, where the two became pages at the royal court. There, Ferdinand took advantage of the most advanced education available in Portugal: he was exposed to religion, writing, mathematics, music and dance, horsemanship, martial arts, algebra, geometry, astronomy, and navigation. Through his privileged position at court, Ferdinand came of age hearing about Portuguese and Spanish discoveries in the Indies, and he learned the secrets of the Portuguese exploration of the ocean. He even assisted with preparing fleets to leave for India, familiarizing himself with provisions, rigging, and arms.

Magellan seemed destined to become a captain himself, but in 1495 his patron, King João, suddenly died. João's successor, Manuel I, mistrusted young Magellan, then still a teenager. As a result, the fast-rising courtier found his career blocked. Although he retained his

Portrait of Ferdinand Magellan painted in the sixteenth century,
believed to be one of the few accurate likenesses of Magellan.

modest position at court, he spent the next decade with no prospect of leading a major expedition for Portugal.

Finally, in 1505, at age twenty-five, Ferdinand Magellan received an assignment aboard a mammoth fleet bound for India. He spent the next eight years trying to establish a permanent Portuguese presence in India, dashing from one trading post to another and from one battle to the next, surviving multiple wounds. If nothing else, he learned to stay alive in a hostile environment.

Magellan displayed remarkable bravery and toughness, but in the end his foreign service proved a mixed adventure. He invested most of his fortune with a merchant who soon died; in the aftermath, Magellan lost most of his assets. He requested compensation from King Manuel, but the king refused. Despite his eight years of service abroad, facing dangers and receiving wounds, Magellan found that his relationship to the court was no better than it had been when he left home.

———————

Magellan, still bristling with ambition, returned to Lisbon and began a new phase in his career. Seeking to make himself useful to the crown, he involved himself with the Portuguese struggle to dominate North Africa. In 1513, he seemed to find an ideal opportunity when the city of Azamor, in Morocco, suddenly refused to pay its annual tribute to Portugal. The Moroccan governor ringed the city with a powerful, well-equipped army. King Manuel responded to the challenge by sending the largest seaborne force ever to sail for his kingdom: five hundred ships, manned by fifteen thousand soldiers—the entire military strength of his small nation.

Among the hordes of soldiers sent to defend the honor of Portugal was Ferdinand Magellan, who brought along an aging horse, the only one he could afford on his drastically reduced budget. He rode courageously into battle, only to lose his horse to the Arabs. What had started so bravely for Magellan turned into a near disaster, as he barely escaped from the siege with his life. The larger picture was more favorable, as

Portugal reclaimed Azamor, but Magellan remained furious. He had lost his horse in the service of his country and king! And the Portuguese army offered him only a fraction of what he considered to be his horse's true value.

Displaying a hotheadedness and tactlessness that would emerge again and again throughout his career, Magellan wrote directly to King Manuel, insulting numerous ministers and insisting on receiving full compensation for the horse. The new request was swiftly dismissed as a minor nuisance.

Magellan's reaction was telling: rather than quitting the field of battle in disgust, he stubbornly remained at his post, somehow acquired a new horse, and participated in skirmishes with the Arabs who swooped out of the desert to harass Portuguese soldiers guarding Azamor. Magellan showed himself to be a fearless warrior, engaging in hand-to-hand combat with the enemy.

In one confrontation, he received a serious wound from an Arab lance, which left him with a shattered knee and a lifelong limp; it also ended his career as a soldier. But at last he received the recognition he craved, for his service in battle earned him a promotion and a share of the spoils.

The reward, however, proved to be his undoing. In a subsequent battle, the Arabs surrendered an immense herd of livestock, which Magellan used to pay off tribal allies. As a result of this transaction, Magellan and another officer were indicted for selling four hundred goats to the enemy and keeping the proceeds for personal gain.

The charges were preposterous. Magellan, as a quartermaster, was entitled to his spoils of war, and it was not clear that he received payment for the beasts. He found the allegations ludicrous and failed to respond to them. Without authorization, he left Morocco for Lisbon, where he appeared before King Manuel. Magellan did not apologize for his action; instead, he demanded an increase in his *moradia*—the allowance he received as a member of the royal household. Making a bad situation even worse, he lectured the king, reminding him that he,

Ferdinand Magellan, was a nobleman who had rendered long service to the crown and had the wounds to show for it.

King Manuel's judgment was swift and sure: Magellan was to return to Morocco immediately to face charges for treason, corruption, and leaving the army without authorization. This he did. After investigating the evidence, a tribunal in Morocco dismissed all charges against him, and he returned to Lisbon clutching a letter of recommendation from his commanding officer. Displaying superhuman stubbornness, Magellan went back to his sovereign king to demand the increased *moradia* with more passion than ever.

Once more, the king refused.

————

Magellan was entering middle age with a bad leg and an unfairly tarnished reputation. Short and dark, and teetering on the brink of poverty, he looked nothing like the aristocrat he thought himself to be. And he still yearned to distinguish himself in the service of Portugal, to make a name for himself that would rank him with the important figures of the day, the explorers who had opened new trade routes for Portugal in the Indies and, in the process, become rich themselves.

It seemed that Magellan was a fool to ask the same king who had refused to increase his *moradia* to back a voyage to the Indies with the goal of discovering a water route to the legendary but little-known Spice Islands—the Moluccas (an archipelago, or group of islands, that is part of modern-day Indonesia)—but the would-be explorer saw matters differently. He was offering the king a scheme, admittedly a bit vague and risky, to fund the crown with the wealth of the Indies. Magellan believed that he could do what his boyhood hero Christopher Columbus had claimed to do but never actually accomplished: reach the Indies by sailing westward across the Atlantic Ocean.

Realizing that he needed help to persuade King Manuel, Magellan brought a well-known figure with him: Ruy Faleiro, who was a cosmographer—a combination of mathematician, astronomer, and

Manuel I of Portugal.

nautical scholar—but was also prone to rapidly changing his mind. When Magellan and Faleiro presented themselves at court with their plan, the king was already prejudiced against the stubborn, defiant Magellan and the volatile Faleiro—both men whose requests he had refused in the past.

Three times, Magellan asked for royal authorization. Three times, the king refused. Finally, in September 1517, Magellan made a clumsy last-ditch attempt to win backing from the Portuguese court. He asked if he could offer his services elsewhere, and, to his astonishment, the king replied that Magellan was free to do as he pleased. When Magellan knelt to kiss the king's hands, as custom dictated, King Manuel concealed them behind his cloak and turned his back on his petitioner.

———

The humiliating rejection proved to be the making of Ferdinand Magellan.

After he received the final rejection from the Portuguese king, the thirty-seven-year-old Magellan suddenly found direction in his life. He moved quickly, carried along by his own ambitions and by the tides of history. By October 20, 1517, he had arrived in Seville, in southwestern Spain. Ruy Faleiro soon joined him there.

Newly arrived mariners from Portugal and Italy such as Magellan found a welcome reception in Spain. Within days of his arrival, Magellan had signed documents formally making him a subject of Castile (the main kingdom of what is now Spain) and its young king, Charles I. No longer was he Fernão de Magalhães; in Spain, he became known as Hernando de Magallanes.

Magellan brought with him to Spain many of Portugal's most precious and sensitive secrets: information about secret expeditions, a familiarity with Portuguese activity in the Indies, and an acquaintance with Portuguese navigational knowledge of the world beyond Europe. But he needed a sponsor.

Brashly, he decided to turn to the court of Spain. His timing was perfect. Spain was trying to catch up to Portugal, the leader in ocean exploration. Charles I was a shy, uncertain eighteen-year-old; he was accustomed to deferring to the bishops who ran the day-to-day affairs of the court, but he was desperate to prove his power. Magellan was an unknown quantity to the Spanish court and ministers. He had renounced his loyalty to Portugal, but he remained an outsider in Spain, on probation and under suspicion. In these difficult circumstances, getting the financial backing for his proposed voyage would require an enormous expenditure of effort and cunning, as well as a generous amount of luck.

Soon after arriving in Seville, Magellan became acquainted with Diogo Barbosa, another Portuguese expatriate. Barbosa had settled in the city fourteen years earlier and was now knight commander of the Order of Santiago. Magellan began to woo Diogo's daughter, Beatriz; the relationship developed very quickly, and they married before the year was out. Suddenly, Magellan had an important sponsor in Seville, as well as a financial stake, because Beatriz brought with her a large dowry. She might have been pregnant at the time of their marriage; a child, named Rodrigo, was born the following year.

Guided by the Barbosa family, Ferdinand Magellan prepared to persuade the powerful Casa de Contratación (House of Commerce) to allow him to undertake his daring voyage. Founded in Seville in 1503 by Queen Isabella, the Casa managed expeditions to the New World on behalf of the Spanish crown. The Casa was controlled by a man who was neither a navigator nor an explorer: Juan Rodríguez de Fonseca, the Bishop of Burgos, a cold, manipulative bureaucrat who jealously guarded his power.

Although Magellan and Fonseca despised one another and fought bitterly, Magellan knew he needed Fonseca's backing in matters of

Charles I of Spain as a young man. He was just eighteen years old when he agreed to commission Magellan's expedition.

exploration because King Charles would do whatever the experienced old Bishop Fonseca recommended.

When Magellan approached representatives of the Casa de Contratación and declared that he believed the Spice Islands were located within the Spanish hemisphere, he was telling them exactly what they wanted to hear. Still, the provisions of the Treaty of Tordesillas posed serious obstacles for the proposed expedition. Members of the Casa failed to see how Magellan could avoid trespassing on Portuguese interests by sailing west until he reached the East. Anticipating this objection, Magellan referred to a clause in the treaty that allowed Spain or Portugal the freedom of the seas to reach lands belonging to one empire or the other.

Then there was the question of Magellan's nationality. The prospect of a Portuguese man leading a Spanish expedition through Portuguese waters made nearly everyone at the Casa de Contratación uneasy; if the Portuguese became aware of the expedition, relations between the two countries might be strained to the breaking point. Yet the Casa's newest member looked at matters quite differently. Juan de Aranda, an ambitious merchant, took the Portuguese navigator aside and offered to lobby on behalf of the expedition in exchange for 20 percent of the profits, a stake that could make him rich beyond imagining.

Aranda wrote enthusiastically on behalf of Magellan, only to be reprimanded by the Casa de Contratación, which reminded him that he was not entitled to negotiate the terms of the expedition. Nevertheless, Aranda arranged a meeting for Magellan with the king's ministers to consider a proposal for an expedition to the Spice Islands. On January 20, 1518, Magellan and Ruy Faleiro set out for Spain's capital city, Valladolid.

————

Magellan came well armed for what would be the most important meeting of his life. To begin, he offered tantalizing letters from his friend Francisco Serrão, a Portuguese explorer, describing the riches of the Spice Islands.

After surviving shipwrecks and pirates, Serrão was among the first Europeans to visit the Spice Islands. Surrounded by the scent of drying cloves, he wrote captivating letters to Magellan from the island of Ternate (in modern-day Indonesia), describing the extravagant beauty and wealth of the Spice Islands. "I beg you to join me here," he wrote in one letter, "that you may sample for yourself the delights that surround me." Serrão cultivated Ternate's small ruling class, especially its king, and tried to promote trade between Ternate and Portugal, but the brisk transoceanic trade that he expected was slow to materialize. Rather than giving up, Serrão stayed on.

Magellan had every intention of visiting Serrão in the island paradise. "God willing," he wrote to his friend, "I will soon be seeing you, whether by way of Portugal or Castile." And when Magellan made a promise, he did everything in his power to keep it.

Serrão's letters placed the Spice Islands far to the east of their true position; he located them squarely within the Spanish hemisphere as defined in the Treaty of Tordesillas. This error might have been intentional, to disguise the Spice Islands' true location from outsiders, but in any event, his geographical manipulation alleviated Spain's principal anxiety: Magellan's expedition to the Spice Islands would not violate the treaty after all.

To dramatize his mission, Magellan displayed his slave, Enrique, who was believed to be a native of the Spice Islands. (This was not quite accurate, but in any event Enrique could act as an interpreter.) After presenting the slave, Magellan spoke excitedly of sailing along the eastern coast of what is now called South America, until the land ended and he was able to turn west toward the Spice Islands. (Magellan's geography proved to be hopelessly distorted.) To clinch his argument, he exhibited a map showing the route he planned to take.

———

Reliable information about trade routes was so sensitive and precious that Magellan's displaying of a stolen Portuguese map was the equivalent of selling nuclear secrets at the height of the Cold War. Magellan's ideas about the world he planned to explore were fatally inaccurate. Without the Pacific Ocean to inform his calculations, the estimated length of his route came to only half the actual distance. Magellan confidently predicted that it would take him two years, at most, to reach the Spice Islands, load his ships with precious cargo, and return to Spain. All he would have to do was find a way to get around or through South America, and he would be at the doorstep of the Indies. The king and his advisers were too intrigued to turn him away. His ideas were big enough, and promised to be lucrative enough, to convince King Charles and his powerful advisers to back them.

Immediately after the meeting at Valladolid, the potential co-leaders of the expedition presented a list of demands to the crown, including an exclusive franchise on the Spice Islands for a full ten years, 5 percent of the rent, and possession of any additional islands they discovered beyond the first six, as well as permission to pass the newly discovered lands on to their "heirs and successors."

—————

On March 22, 1518, King Charles offered Magellan and Faleiro a charter to discover a new world on behalf of Spain. King Charles appeared to give Magellan a ten-year exclusive. In the event, he did not honor this promise: Charles would dispatch a follow-up expedition to the Spice Islands only six years after Magellan's departure from Spain. The Spice Islands were too valuable, and too strategically important, to entrust to a single explorer.

King Charles instructed Magellan and Faleiro to respect Portugal's territorial rights under the terms of the Treaty of Tordesillas, "except within the limits of our demarcation." He reminded Magellan of the delicate diplomatic and family situation complicating the rivalry of Spain and Portugal for mastery of the seas and of world trade. Portugal's sovereign, King Manuel, had married not just one but *two* of Charles's aunts, first Isabel and then, after Isabel's death, María. Now that María had also died, Manuel was planning to marry Charles's sister, Leonor, within a matter of weeks.

From Magellan's standpoint, this was a remarkable contract because it gave him nearly everything he had wanted. From Fonseca's point of view, it gave Magellan too much money and too much power over the expedition. It would take Fonseca months, but eventually he would have his revenge on Magellan.

———

King Charles promised Magellan five ships. The fleet would be called the Armada de Molucca, after the Indonesian name for the Spice Islands. The ships were the most complicated machines of their day, wonders of Renaissance technology and the products of thousands of hours of labor by skilled artisans working at their specialized trades. The ships were mostly black—pitch black. Their blackness, which gave them an ominous aura, came from the tar covering their hulls, masts, and rigging—practically every exposed surface except for the sails. Their sterns rose high out of the water, towering up to thirty feet over the waves, so high that a man standing on the stern deck seemed to rule the sea itself.

———

In a final piece of official business, King Charles gave the title of captain to both Magellan and Faleiro. Given the hazards of exploration, it was not unusual for expeditions in the Age of Discovery to have co-captains, but in this case the arrangement unintentionally sowed the seeds of bitter disputes at sea. The powers granted to the pair were sweeping. Magellan and Faleiro would have absolute authority over everyone else involved with the expedition. "We authorize you," wrote Charles (using the royal "we"), "to execute sentence on their persons and goods. . . . If during the voyage . . . there should arise any disputes and conflicts, at sea as well as ashore, you shall deliver, determine and render justice with respect to them, summarily and without hesitation nor question of law."

Magellan could only have marveled at the speed with which his plan to reach the Spice Islands had come together. King Charles risked Spain's authority and reputation on the expedition, but Magellan would risk even more: his very life.

CHAPTER TWO
THE MAN WITHOUT
A COUNTRY

W hen word of Magellan's spectacular commission reached
Portugal, King Manuel was alarmed. The navigator had
betrayed them all, and the members of the royal court were unwilling
to point out why. No one in Portugal dared to admit the reason for
Magellan's behavior—that King Manuel had refused to back the
navigator, humiliating him not once but four times.

King Manuel did what he could to ruin Magellan's name while at
the same time trying to lure Magellan and Faleiro back to Portugal. He
asked the Portuguese ambassador to King Charles's court, Álvaro da
Costa, to track down the two exiles to inform them that King Manuel
was willing to reconsider. Da Costa bluntly explained to Magellan the
serious consequences he faced if he continued with his plan to sail
for Spain: he would offend not only King Manuel but also God, and
he would give up all personal honor. Matters wouldn't end there; his
family and heirs would suffer, and he would upset the delicate truce
between Spain and Portugal at the very moment King Manuel was
planning to marry King Charles's sister, Leonor.

Magellan refused to be swayed. He suspected that if he returned to
Portugal he would be thrown into jail, tried for treason, and executed.
Summoning his meager diplomatic skills, Magellan replied that he had
formally renounced his allegiance to King Manuel and given his loyalty
to King Charles. He had no obligation to serve anyone else.

———

Under pressure from Portugal to cancel the expedition and uncertain
about how to handle the situation, King Charles turned to his advisers
for guidance. They restated their position that the Spice Islands lay in

the Spanish hemisphere and that Magellan's expedition would not violate the Treaty of Tordesillas. King Charles followed their advice, and Magellan and Faleiro retained his backing.

Despite all the tension between Portugal and Spain, King Manuel agreed to marry Charles I's sister, Leonor. Rivals for the control of world trade would be yoked together by marriage. Four days after King Manuel completed his nuptial arrangements with King Charles, the Spanish monarch instructed the Casa de Contratación to proceed with Magellan's expedition to the Spice Islands without delay. Magellan and Faleiro were given money to begin their preparations, and they were ordered to go to Seville to outfit their ships.

––––––––

Seville, at the height of the Age of Discovery, hovered at the peak of its wealth and influence in 1518. The city straddling the Guadalquivir River was a blend of Roman, Visigothic, Muslim, Jewish, and Christian cultures. Its fame echoed throughout the known world, borne on ships to destinations only vaguely located on maps.

Above all, Seville was a commercial center. Only Seville was capable of providing Magellan with the technology, the labor, the motivation, and the financial resources to travel halfway around the world in search of lands to claim and spices to bring back to Europe.

When Magellan and Faleiro arrived in Seville to begin preparations for the voyage, rumors circulated that the lives of the Portuguese co-commanders were in serious danger. Magellan ignored the death threats, but King Charles took the intimidation so seriously that he provided bodyguards for Magellan and Faleiro, granted them another audience, and declared them Knights of the Order of Santiago. Having done all he could to demonstrate his support of the two Portuguese men, King Charles urged them to begin their expedition as soon as possible. Time was short, and an empire was at stake.

––––––––

"Something has come up," Magellan wrote to King Charles on Saturday, October 23, 1518, in the midst of outfitting the fleet for

The bustling port of Seville on the Guadalquivir River, painted in the sixteenth century.

the voyage. Unlike many captains, Magellan involved himself in the day-to-day preparations, even loading goods onto the ships as if he were an ordinary seaman, not the captain general.

Magellan explained, "I ordered the men to put up four flags with my coat of arms . . . while those of Your Majesty were to be placed on top of *Trinidad*, which is the name of the ship." The unusual juxtaposition of signs, advertising that a Portuguese captain was sailing for Spain, attracted a large, gossipy crowd of onlookers. The crowd thought the four flags bearing Magellan's coat of arms represented the king of Portugal. Their resentment boiled along until a functionary ordered Magellan to remove the offending flags. Another Spanish official approached Magellan with the same demand. No, Magellan explained, he would not take down the flags.

Chaos erupted. The two officials who had challenged Magellan got into a fight with each other over how to treat him. The workmen repairing *Trinidad* quickly fled, as did a number of the sailors, further upsetting Magellan, who stood by helplessly as he watched the local officials disarm the sailors and even arrest several of them and lead them away to prison. In the struggle, one of Magellan's pilots was stabbed as he was going about his work. Although Magellan was unharmed, his dignity and authority had suffered tremendous blows. To make matters worse, the fight had occurred in the open, under the watchful eye of a Portuguese spy, who would carry news of the brawl back to Lisbon.

Magellan's fury was understandable. On paper, he enjoyed the protection of King Charles, but in reality he was at the mercy of the mob. If he could not maintain order here on the quay at Seville, how would he lead men on the dangerous journey across an uncharted ocean to the Spice Islands? And if there was an uprising on a distant shore, where it would be impossible for him to summon the king's help, what would happen then?

Within days of receiving Magellan's letter, King Charles demonstrated his loyalty and punished the offenders. Preparations for the voyage continued, but the flag incident served as a warning to Magellan that his men, especially the Spaniards, posed a danger as great as the sea itself.

———————

On April 6, 1519, the king sent orders to another officer, Juan de Cartagena, to serve as the inspector general of the fleet under the two Portuguese commanders. These orders became the most controversial aspect of the entire expedition. Essentially, Cartagena was to have the final say over all commercial aspects of the expedition; he was the chief accountant and representative of the king's treasury.

It would be Cartagena's job to check every entry in every book and, once it met his approval, sign off on it. And it was certainly in his interest to do so, because he had invested his own funds in the expedition. This provision made Magellan responsible to Cartagena for all commercial decisions.

There was more. Cartagena was to function as the eyes and ears of the king throughout the voyage. If the co-commanders were careless in any way, Cartagena was to inform the Casa de Contratación in writing. The instructions were so thorough that one could say Cartagena had the final say on the entire voyage.

And that was exactly the conclusion to which Cartagena came.

———————

On May 8, 1519, during frantic preparations for departure, King Charles delivered his final instructions for the voyage to Magellan and Faleiro. The instructions were so detailed it was as if the king were coming along in one of the ships.

Magellan and Faleiro were ordered to record every landfall and landmark they reached. They were also to treat humanely any indigenous peoples they happened to find, if only to make it possible for the fleet to ensure its supply of food and water. Magellan could seize any Arabs he found in the Portuguese hemisphere—hinting that he might violate the Treaty of Tordesillas, after all—and, if he wished, sell them as slaves.

In contrast, if Magellan came across Arabs in the Spanish hemisphere, he was to treat them well and to make treaties with their leaders. Magellan was to go in search of spices and lands, and nothing else, and when he reached the Spice Islands, he was to "make a treaty of peace or commerce with the king or lord of that land" before he attempted to load the goods onto his ships.

And on a sensitive point, Magellan and Faleiro had to make sure the crew members had no contact with local women. Another clause prohibited the use of firearms; members of the expedition were forbidden to discharge them in newly found lands to avoid terrifying the Indians on whose goodwill they would depend.

————

Since leaving Portugal—and even before, as King Manuel had noted— Ruy Faleiro, the brilliant cosmographer, had shown signs of instability. People remarked on his irritability and lack of sleep. Some thought he had simply lost his mind.

Even King Charles took note of Faleiro's condition, and on July 26, 1519, issued a royal certificate declaring that Faleiro would not sail with Magellan. Instead, the cosmographer would remain in Seville to prepare for another expedition that would follow in Magellan's wake.

Magellan seemed relieved to rid himself of Faleiro; he agreed to the removal as long as the fleet could keep the cosmographer's precious, state-of-the-art navigational instruments. Faleiro's collection consisted of compasses, a wooden astrolabe, and charts—twenty-four in all, most of them top secret, all of them extremely valuable. An unauthorized individual caught with a chart could be punished severely, even put to death. The charts were kept under lock and key, and under armed guard. All of the instruments remained with the armada, at Magellan's disposal. The fleet also carried prepared blank parchment, as well as dried skins to make still more parchment, if necessary, for additional maps.

Fonseca, who had recently become an archbishop, replaced the cosmographer Faleiro with Andrés de San Martín, a well-connected Spanish cosmographer and astronomer who aspired to be part of the

Casa. Cartagena, the inspector general, took Faleiro's place as co-commander. From Fonseca's point of view, the promotion contained a certain numerical logic because the expedition would now have one Spanish and one Portuguese leader, but Magellan did not view matters that way. He considered himself the sole captain general and Cartagena the inspector general, not a co-admiral.

Cartagena was referred to as Fonseca's nephew; in reality, he was Fonseca's illegitimate son. So although he had no experience at sea, and no qualifications to recommend him as a captain, Juan de Cartagena found himself leading one of the largest Spanish maritime expeditions to date. Not only that, but Fonseca appointed two close friends as captains of two of the ships: Luis de Mendoza, who assumed command of *Victoria*, and Gaspar de Quesada, of *Concepción*. All three captains appointed by Fonseca—Cartagena, Quesada, and Mendoza—looked down on Magellan from the moment they came on board.

Here, at last, was Fonseca's revenge on Magellan. No matter what the contract said, Fonseca had managed to suppress Magellan's authority, and potentially his share of the proceeds of the expedition, by appointing his natural son and his close allies to virtually all the other important positions in the armada. These appointments set the stage for endless challenges to Magellan's authority—and ultimately for mutiny.

———

After Fonseca removed Faleiro, he turned his attention to Juan de Aranda, who had first introduced Magellan to the Castilian court. Fonseca launched an investigation into Aranda's business arrangements with Magellan and Faleiro. All three were questioned separately. Under oath, Magellan described the fees Aranda had received for the services he provided the explorers.

The Supreme Council faulted Aranda for his actions, declaring that he had committed a criminal act by receiving money from Magellan; the judgment was signed by the council's president, who just happened to be Fonseca. Two weeks later, the Spanish crown removed Aranda from any further involvement with the expedition. He was disgraced. Magellan could only wonder what the all-powerful Fonseca might do next to the Armada de Molucca.

————

As the date of departure approached, the ships took on all the sailing gear, arms, provisions, and furnishings the crew would need for the voyage. Magellan approached the task of provisioning with as much attention to detail as he did the outfitting of the ships, and with good reason: food was a costly investment—nearly as costly as the entire fleet. There was just enough to get the sailors through the first leg or two of the voyage, which meant they would be looking for additional food at almost every port, and in the ocean itself.

Nearly four-fifths of the armada's food supply consisted of just two items: wine and hardtack. Hardtack, a staple of the sailor's diet, was made of coarse wheat flour, including the husk, kneaded with hot water (never cold), and cooked twice. The result, a brittle yet tough biscuit, was stored for up to a month before it was sold. The ships also held flour stored in wooden barrels, to be kneaded with seawater and grilled as a kind of tortilla, as well as meat, usually pork, bacon, ham, and especially salted beef. More meat would come from seven cows and three pigs; their presence turned the ship that carried them into a floating barn, with an odor to match.

Barrels of cheese, almonds in the shell, mustard, and casks of figs were also loaded on board the ships. As unlikely as it sounds, Magellan's fleet carried fish—sardines, cod, anchovies, and tuna—all of it dried and salted. Expecting to catch fresh fish along their route, Magellan stored a generous amount of fishing line and lots of hooks in the ships' holds. There was little in the way of fresh vegetables. All fruit was preserved.

The officers brought with them a delicacy: a jam made from quince, a small, hard, apple-like fruit. As the voyage progressed, quince jam would play a crucial role in the lives of the sailors, and in Magellan's as well.

The provisions made for an unhealthy diet, high in salt, low in protein, and lacking essential vitamins that sailors needed to protect themselves against the rigors of the sea.

————

Arguments over the crew's nationalities and pay plagued Magellan until the moment the fleet left Seville. The Casa de Contratación ordered Magellan to limit his entire crew to 235 men, including cabin boys, and gave him official permission to hire only 12 Portuguese; in reality he was taking nearly 40 with him. Magellan pleaded in writing with the Casa to allow the men he had hired to board the ships, regardless of nationality. If he could not have the crew he wanted, he would abandon the expedition.

On the day before his departure, August 9, 1519, Magellan was summoned to testify that he had made every effort to hire Spanish officers and crew members rather than foreigners. Qualified sailors were rare in Seville, Magellan argued, and qualified sailors willing to risk their lives on a voyage to the Spice Islands rarer still. Although he did not say so, few Spanish seamen wanted to sail under a Portuguese captain.

Although he kept positions for at least two of his own relatives—Álvaro de Mesquita, his first cousin on his mother's side, and Cristóvão Rebêlo, his illegitimate son—he did give up three other relatives he had quietly enlisted. These last-minute compromises pacified the Casa, and the captain general received the final blessing for his expedition. After twelve months of painstaking preparation, the Armada de Molucca was at last ready to conquer the ocean.

————

Just before departure, the officers and crew of the five ships comprising the fleet, 260 strong, attended a solemn mass at the convent of Santa María de la Victoria, located in Triana, the sailors' district of Seville.

During the ceremony, King Charles's representative presented Magellan with the royal flag as the captain general knelt before an

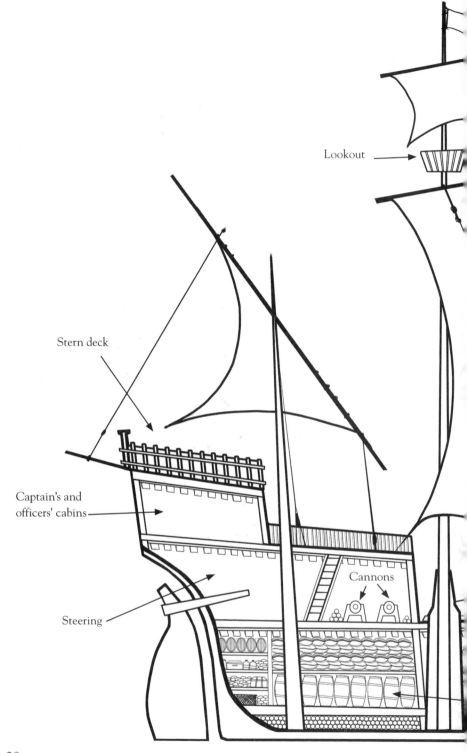

Lookout

Stern deck

Captain's and
officers' cabins

Cannons

Steering

Cross-section of a typical Spanish ship of the early sixteenth century, similar to Magellan's flagship, *Trinidad*. No drawings, paintings, or plans of the actual ships of the Armada de Molucca survive.

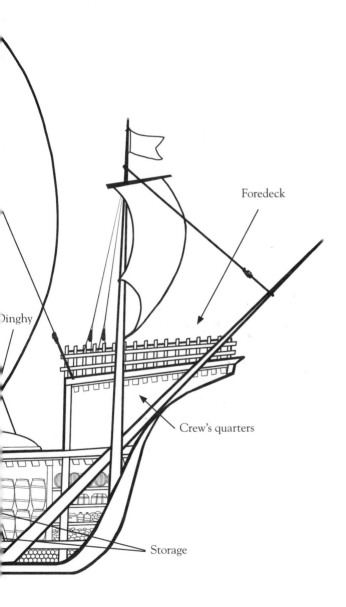

Foredeck

Dinghy

Crew's quarters

Storage

image of the Virgin Mary. This marked the first occasion the king had ever given the royal colors to a non-Castilian.

Still kneeling, his head bent, Magellan swore that he was the king's faithful servant and that he would fulfill all his obligations to guarantee the success of the expedition. When he was finished, the captains repeated the oath and swore to obey Magellan and to follow him on his route, wherever it might lead.

Among those in attendance at Santa María de la Victoria that day was an Italian scholar named Antonio Pigafetta, who had spent long years in the service of an emissary to Pope Leo X. Pigafetta, about thirty years old at the time, was a man of learning (he boasted of having "read many books") and religious conviction, but he also had a thirst for adventure, or, as he put it, "a craving for experience and glory."

When he heard about Magellan's expedition to the Spice Islands, Pigafetta felt destiny calling. During the next several months, he helped gather navigational instruments and gained Magellan's trust. Pigafetta quickly came to idolize the captain general, despite their differing nationalities, and was awestruck by the ambitiousness and danger of the mission. Pigafetta decided he had to go along. Although he lacked experience at sea, he did have both funds and papal credentials.

Magellan, who left nothing to accident, had an assignment for Pigafetta: the young Italian diplomat was to keep a record of the voyage—not the usual dry, factual pilot's log, but a more personal, anecdotal, and free-flowing account in the tradition of other popular travel works of the day. Such reports included a book by Magellan's brother-in-law, Duarte Barbosa, and one by Marco Polo, the most celebrated Italian traveler of them all.

From the moment the fleet left Seville, Pigafetta kept a diary of events that gradually evolved from a routine depiction of life at sea to a shockingly graphic and candid diary that serves as the best record of the voyage. He took his role as the expedition's official chronicler seriously, and his descriptions burst with botanical, linguistic, and anthropological detail.

Magellan's departure deeply affected the lives of those he left behind. His wife, Beatriz, pregnant with their second child, lived quietly under the protection of her father. Although she received a monthly salary, as specified in Magellan's contract, she was, in fact, a hostage to the Spanish authorities. If word should reach Seville that Magellan had done anything troublesome during the expedition or was disloyal to King Charles, she would be the first person the king's agents would seek out.

Magellan realized he might die far from home, in a part of the world that was still a blank on European maps. In his will, he stated: "I desire that if I die in this city of Seville my body may be buried in the Monastery of Santa María de la Victoria in Triana—ward and precinct of the city of Seville—in the grave set apart for me; and if I die on this said voyage, I desire that my body may be buried in a church dedicated to Our Lady, in the nearest spot at which death seize me and I die." He made certain that all of his acknowledged family members would be well taken care of. He specified that Beatriz's entire dowry be returned to her; that his illegitimate son, Cristóvão Rebêlo, whom he called "my page," receive an inheritance; and that his slave, Enrique, be freed and given a generous sum of money.

Thinking he would be leaving behind a great empire, Magellan willed to Rodrigo, his legitimate son, along with any other legitimate male heirs that he might have, all the rights and titles King Charles had granted to him for the voyage to the Spice Islands. He hoped Rodrigo and the child Beatriz was then carrying might grow up to find themselves the rulers of distant lands administered by Spain, and very wealthy rulers at that.

The Portuguese reacted bitterly to the upcoming departure of the Armada de Molucca. King Manuel ordered the harassment of Magellan's relatives who remained in their homeland. To make Magellan's dishonor public, vandals were sent to the family estate in Sabrosa; they tore the Magellan escutcheon from the gates and smashed it to the ground, and they even threw stones at young relatives of Magellan. Fearing for their lives, Magellan's relatives fled the country. Abandoned, the Sabrosa estate fell into ruin, and another house rose on the site. The stone that once held the Magellan family crest met with a special fate: it was covered with feces.

CHAPTER THREE

—— NEVERLANDS ——

"On the tenth of August," Antonio Pigafetta recorded in his diary, "the fleet, having been furnished with all that was necessary for it and having in the five ships people of divers[e] nations to the number of two hundred and thirty-seven in all, was ready to depart from . . . Seville, and firing all the artillery we set sail with the staysail only."

To reach the Atlantic, the five ships—*Trinidad, San Antonio, Concepción, Santiago,* and *Victoria*—negotiated the winding Guadalquivir River, whose hazards tested the pilots' abilities. Hidden sandbanks, the hulls of shipwrecks, and shallow areas lurked beneath the river's murky waters, and occasionally these obstacles spelled disaster for an expedition even before it reached the open sea.

Adding to the tension, everyone aboard the ships knew Moorish pirates still patrolled the Spanish coast, looking for ships loaded with precious resources and, most of all, weapons—ships like those of the Armada de Molucca.

———

A week after leaving Seville, the fleet reached the mouth of the Guadalquivir River and the snug coastal town of Sanlúcar de Barrameda, the final point of departure. On arrival, the crew found a windswept seaport, perched on the edge of the world, bustling with a sense of adventure.

Beyond the crowded town lay the churning waters of the Atlantic. To Magellan and his crew, the body of water was known simply as the Ocean Sea, believed to girdle the globe. Many ships had departed from Sanlúcar de Barrameda, and some had been fortunate enough to return from distant ports and newly discovered lands, but none had circumnavigated the entire world.

To assert his absolute authority over his resentful captains, Magellan gave strict sailing orders. Although strict, they were "good and honorable regulations," in Pigafetta's words, and consistent with procedures followed by other fleets of the era. "First," Pigafetta noted, "the said captain general desired that his ship should go before the other ships and that the others should follow him." If the flagship, *Trinidad*, signaled, the others were to reply; that way, Magellan could tell if his fleet was following him. If the watchman suddenly discovered land or even a reef, Magellan would display lights or fire a mortar.

Magellan's procedures demanded discipline from an inexperienced crew lacking respect for the captain general. The least offensive standing order—the requirement that all ships report to *Trinidad* at dusk—irritated the crew the most, because it demonstrated that Magellan, and no one else, served as the leader of the Armada de Molucca.

————

Leaving Sanlúcar de Barrameda on September 20, 1519, the five ships of the armada plunged into the Atlantic Ocean. Amid the complex, choreographed flurry of activity aboard the ships, officers shouted orders, but their words at this crucial moment sounded more like prayers than commands. Juan de Escalante de Mendoza, an experienced Spanish seaman, described the scene: "If the special pilot for the sandbar said that it was time to make sail, the ship's pilot would call out the following to the two men aloft on the yard: 'Ease the rope of the foresail, in the name of the Holy Trinity, Father, and Son, and Holy Spirit, three persons in one single true God, that they may be with us and give us good and safe voyage, and carry us and return us safely to our homes!'"

With those words ringing in their ears, the sailors hauled the hemp ropes holding anchors, set the sails, and felt the breeze freshen against their faces. The ships picked up speed, and the coastline began to recede; there was no turning back now. The voyage would sustain them all, or it would destroy them all. To reach his goal, Magellan would have to master both the great Ocean Sea and a sea of ignorance.

It was a dream as old as the imagination: a voyage to the ends of the earth. Yet until the Age of Discovery, it remained only a dream. Magellan undertook his ambitious voyage in a world ruled by superstition, populated with strange and demonic creatures, and reverberating with a longing for religious redemption. To the average person, the world beyond Europe was like one of the fantastic realms depicted in *The Thousand and One Nights*, a collection of Middle Eastern and Indian tales, including "The Seven Voyages of Sinbad the Sailor." Going to

A modern replica of Victoria *under sail.* Victoria *would be the only one of Magellan's ships to complete the circumnavigation and return to Spain.*

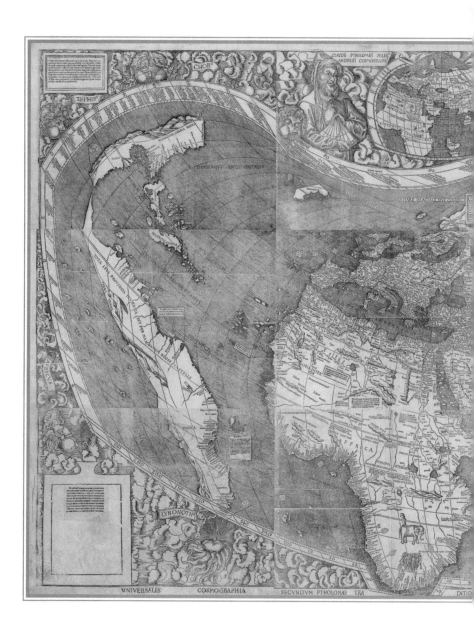

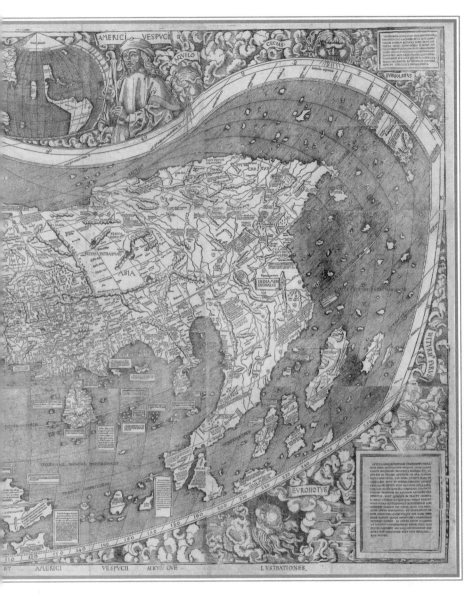

The European view of the world before Magellan's voyage.
This 1507 map by Martin Waldseemüller shows the eastern coast of the Americas,
but omits the Pacific Ocean and the Strait of Magellan.

sea was the most adventurous thing one could do—the Renaissance equivalent of becoming an astronaut—but the likelihood of death and disaster was far greater. These days, there are no undiscovered places on earth; in the age of the global positioning system, no one need get lost. But in the Age of Discovery, people believed that sea monsters lurked in the briny depths, waiting to devour those who dared to cross the ocean. Even mariners believed that when they crossed the equator, the ocean would boil and scald them to death.

————

Fair weather favored the Armada de Molucca, and gusts carried the black ships southwest to the Canary Islands, off the coast of northwestern Africa. During a brief stay in the Canaries, Magellan busied himself with the final provisioning of his fleet. He worked quickly—too quickly, as he would later discover. The chandlers (maritime merchants) of the Canary Islands had exaggerated the amount of supplies they sold to the fleet, and what they did sell was in poor condition. This type of cheating was common, and very dangerous to the expeditions whose lives depended on the food purchased in the Canaries.

After three busy days in a harbor on Tenerife, the largest of the Canary Islands, Pigafetta wrote, "We departed thence and came to a port called Monterose, where we remained two days to furnish ourselves with pitch, which is a thing very necessary for ships."

While there, Magellan heard disturbing news: King Manuel of Portugal had dispatched not one but two fleets of caravels (light, quick ships developed by the Portuguese) and ordered their crews to arrest him—a drastic measure. Magellan also received a secret communiqué from his father-in-law, Diogo Barbosa, warning that the Castilian captains in the Armada de Molucca planned to mutiny at the very first chance. They might even kill Magellan. "Keep a good watch," Barbosa warned. The ringleader's name came as no surprise to Magellan: Juan de Cartagena, the Castilian with blood ties to Archbishop Fonseca.

Under the circumstances, Magellan decided that the best course of action was to keep the warnings to himself and leave the Canaries immediately. If the Portuguese caravels caught up with Magellan, they would return him in shackles to the Portuguese court, where he would be convicted of treason, tortured, and perhaps executed. Poorly provisioned but afraid for his life and the welfare of the fleet, Magellan gave the order to raise anchor and set sail at midnight, October 3.

Magellan attempted to place as much distance as possible between his ships and the Portuguese caravels. He also plotted a new, unexpected route that would be difficult for the Portuguese to follow. He led the fleet southwest, hugging the coast of Africa, rather than west across the Atlantic. From the deck of *San Antonio*, following closely behind the flagship, Cartagena challenged Magellan's orders. Why, he demanded, was Magellan following this unusual route?

Follow and do not ask questions, instructed the captain general.

Cartagena insisted Magellan should have consulted his captains and pilots. Was he trying to get them all killed by following this dangerous course? Magellan did not attempt to explain; he simply reminded the other captains to follow.

For the next fifteen days, the Armada de Molucca ran before the wind; the favorable conditions gave Magellan time to strategize about the best way to avoid his Portuguese pursuers. Although he had seen no evidence of them, he continued to follow the coast of Africa rather than head west. But as they worked their way farther south, the weather turned. During most of November, the fleet battled strong headwinds and treacherous gales.

They had no reliable nautical charts, no indications of rocks or other hazards, and no idea when the miserable weather would change for the better. Cooking fires were extinguished, the men went without sleep, and life on board the battered vessels became exceedingly hazardous. One slip, and a sailor could plunge into the sea without hope of rescue.

Throughout the ordeal, sharks circled the ships, terrifying the crew.

———————

After weeks of constant, life-threatening storms, several hissing, glowing globes mysteriously appeared on the yardarms of Magellan's ship, *Trinidad*. Saint Elmo's fire! This dramatic electrical discharge looks like a stream of fire as it trails from the mast of a ship; it can even surround someone's head, causing an eerie tingling sensation. The superstitious sailors, always alert to omens, associated the phenomenon with Saint Peter Gonzalez, a Dominican priest who was considered the patron saint of mariners and who had acquired the name Saint Elmo; the "fire" was viewed as a sign of his protection.

To the terrified, storm-tossed crew, Saint Elmo's fire assumed "the form of a lighted torch at the height of the maintop, and remained there more than two hours and a half, to the comfort of us all. For we were in tears, expecting only the hour of death. And when this holy light was about to leave us, it was so bright to the eyes of all that we were for more than a quarter of an hour as blind as men calling for mercy. For without any doubt, no man thought he would escape from that storm."

Some crew members believed that supernatural powers had singled out the captain general for a special destiny. But their relief from the dangers of the sea was brief, and Magellan's ability to save them would soon be tested again.

CHAPTER FOUR
"THE CHURCH OF THE LAWLESS"

Sixty days of furious storms left the ships of the Armada de Molucca in need of repair and ruined a good part of the precious food supply. Magellan decided it was necessary to reduce rations. Each man received only four pints of drinking water a day, and half that amount of wine. The hardtack ration was also reduced to a pound and a half a day. As with his other decisions, Magellan did not explain why he was reducing the amount of food and drink.

After the gales ended, the battered black ships drifted into equatorial calms, where they rode helplessly in the water. The rebellious Spanish captains, with time on their hands, resumed plotting against the captain general.

One day Magellan advised his crew that the captain of each ship was to approach *Trinidad* at dusk to pay his respects to Magellan and to receive orders. This was Cartagena's chance to act. When *San Antonio* approached the flagship, the quartermaster rather than Cartagena spoke up and, worse, refused to address Magellan by the correct title. Cartagena should have said, *"Dios vos salve, señor capitán-general, y maestro y buena campaña."* ("God keep you, sir captain general and master, and good company.") Instead, the lowly quartermaster called Magellan "captain" rather than "captain general."

Magellan sharply reminded Cartagena of the proper form of address, but the Castilian captain took the opportunity to insult Magellan again. If Magellan did not approve of *San Antonio*'s quartermaster offering the ceremonial salute, Cartagena would happily select a lowly page next time. For several days after that exchange, Cartagena neglected all forms of salute. Magellan had to plan an effective way to handle

Cartagena's rebellious attitude or risk losing control over the entire fleet.

———

Magellan held a tense meeting with the other captains of the fleet in his cabin; there was Juan de Cartagena from *San Antonio*, Gaspar de Quesada from *Concepción*, Luis de Mendoza from *Victoria*, and Juan Rodríguez Serrano from *Santiago*. Magellan realized all the captains except Serrano were determined to lead a mutiny. Cartagena immediately began attacking Magellan about the peculiar and dangerous course they had been following along the coast of Africa.

First, Cartagena complained, Magellan had led them into storms and now he had gotten them trapped in equatorial calms. Cartagena insisted that the only explanation for this bizarre behavior was that Magellan intended to sabotage the fleet, because no matter how loyal to King Charles he claimed to be, Magellan's true loyalty belonged with King Manuel.

Another resentment fueled Cartagena's passion for mutiny: he believed that King Charles had appointed him co-admiral of the fleet along with Magellan. As a Castilian loyal to his sovereign, Cartagena declared he would no longer take orders from Magellan.

Fully prepared to counter Cartagena's challenge, the captain general gave a sign, and Gonzalo Gómez de Espinosa, *Trinidad*'s *alguacil* (master-at-arms), stormed the cabin. Right behind him came two loyalists, Duarte Barbosa and Cristóvão Rebêlo, with swords drawn. Magellan leaped at Cartagena, catching the Castilian by the ruff of his shirt, and shoved him into a chair. "Rebel!" Magellan shouted, "This is mutiny! You are my prisoner, in the king's name."

At that, Cartagena barked at the other disloyal captains, Quesada and Mendoza, to stab Magellan with their daggers. From the way he spoke, it was clear that the three of them had plotted to overthrow the captain general, but now, at the crucial moment, they lost their will to act.

Seizing the initiative, Espinosa picked up Cartagena and shoved him out of the captain's cabin to the main deck, where he was secured to stocks intended for common seamen who had committed minor offenses. Seeing a Castilian officer subjected to this humiliation was more than Quesada and Mendoza could bear. They pleaded with Magellan to free Cartagena or at least to release him into their custody. They reminded their captain general that they had demonstrated their loyalty by ignoring Cartagena. They persuaded Magellan that he had nothing to fear from them, and he agreed to free Cartagena on the condition that Mendoza confine him aboard *Victoria*. Cartagena was immediately relieved of command.

Had he chosen, Magellan could have organized a court martial and sentenced Cartagena to death. As captain general, he would have been within his rights, because Cartagena had plotted to kill Magellan; nothing could be more serious. But Magellan was very aware of Cartagena's privileged position and erred on the side of caution.

With the mutiny at an end, Magellan ordered the trumpets aboard the flagship to sound, alerting the other ships. He then announced that the fleet's accountant, Antonio de Coca, would command *San Antonio*.

Stripped of his command, and having learned nothing from the experience of his failed mutiny, Cartagena burned with desire for revenge against Magellan, no matter what the cost to the expedition—and as Fonseca's son, Cartagena had the power to make great trouble. Of all the dangers Magellan faced on the journey's first leg, the greatest was Cartagena's betrayal.

———

With Cartagena removed from power, Magellan turned his attention to his long-delayed crossing of the Atlantic. For three weeks in late October and November, the fleet headed south, awaiting trade winds. At last the sails began to fill, and Magellan ordered the ships to set a southwesterly course toward South America. Learning that *Concepción*'s pilot, João Lopes Carvalho, had visited several years before on an earlier expedition, Magellan brought him over to *Trinidad* to serve as pilot.

Finally, on December 13, 1519, the fleet entered the lush and gorgeous bay then known to the Portuguese as Rio de Janeiro (modern-day Guanabara Bay). *Trinidad* went first, slipping past Sugarloaf Mountain and coming quietly to anchor in the harbor. Magellan had arrived in the New World.

————

The arrival of the Armada de Molucca in Rio de Janeiro coincided with heavy rains that ended a two-month drought in the region. "The day we arrived the rain began," Pigafetta noted, "so that the people of the place said that we came from heaven and had brought the rain with us." The sight of strange ships arriving in the harbor inspired peaceful feelings in the hearts of the Indians, as Pigafetta later learned. "They thought that the small boats of the ships were the children of the ships, and that the said ships gave birth to them when the boats were lowered to send the men hither and yon."

As Magellan's ships came to rest, a throng of women swam out to greet them. Deprived of the company of women for months, the sailors believed they had found an earthly paradise. Discovering that the women were for sale, the sailors gladly exchanged their cheap German knives for companionship.

One of Magellan's most trusted allies, Duarte Barbosa, who had offered critical assistance when Cartagena mutinied, all but lost his head in Rio de Janeiro. Falling under the women's spell and imagining a life of ease as a trader on these distant shores, he decided to desert the fleet. Magellan learned of the plan and intervened at the last minute, sending sailors to arrest Barbosa onshore and drag him back to the ships. The poor man spent the rest of the layover in Rio de Janeiro confined in shackles aboard his ship, gazing on the women and the self-indulgent life that Magellan—and duty—had denied him.

While the sailors spent time with the Indian women, Magellan conducted business with their men. He took on fresh supplies of water and provisions, trading such insignificant trinkets as tiny bells that he had brought with him from Seville in exchange for precious food.

Five days later, in the shelter of Rio's harbor, the Armada de Molucca observed its first Christmas away from Spain. But there was little time to reflect on the holiday, because the men were busily preparing the ships for departure.

Just before sailing, Magellan replaced Antonio de Coca, who had briefly assumed command of *San Antonio* from Cartagena, with the inexperienced Álvaro de Mesquita. Both Coca and Cartagena were insulted and cried nepotism, which was quite literally true, because Mesquita was Magellan's cousin. The lack of qualified captains in the fleet's roster would trouble Magellan throughout the voyage.

The fleet's departure became emotionally charged. João Carvalho, Magellan's pilot, returning to Brazil after a seven-year absence, happily reunited with his former Brazilian mistress, who introduced him to their son. Carvalho took an immediate liking to the lad, whom he called Joãozito, and enlisted him as a servant aboard ship. As the fleet prepared to go on board, he begged Magellan for permission to take along the mother of his child, but Magellan allowed absolutely no women on the ships. When the fleet finally sailed away, Indian women followed them in canoes, tearfully pleading with the men from distant shores to stay with them forever.

On December 27, the ships finally weighed anchor and departed Rio de Janeiro, turning south down the South American coastline in search of a strait that would take them to Asia and the Spice Islands.

Four months from Seville, the crew and officers had become familiar with the ships as well as the hardships of life at sea. They had learned of the violence of storms and the limits of the proud vessels in which they sailed over the surface of the limitless ocean. The misery of seasickness was at last behind them.

At sea, sleep became the ultimate luxury; a deep sleep was nearly impossible to come by. The crew took naps whenever they could, night or day. Exhausted sailors found a plank or, better still, a sheltered area of the deck where they could sprawl. They eased the wood's bruising hardness with a straw pallet, and they shielded themselves against the cold and wet with heavy blankets. Even then, they couldn't get comfortable.

The men never became accustomed to the rich variety of unpleasant odors brewing aboard their ships. Water seeping into the hold stank despite the efforts to disinfect it with vinegar; the cows and pigs added to the reek, as did the slowly rotting food supply and the sickening smell of salted fish wafting from the hold.

Pests were everywhere. Shipworms (not actually worms, but rather a species of saltwater clam) bored through the hull, slowly compromising the seaworthiness of the entire vessel; one ship in Magellan's fleet eventually disintegrated because of the wretched little creatures. Rats and mice infested every ship, and the sailors learned to live with them and even to play with them. It is recorded that the men of the Armada de Molucca were plagued with all manner of lice, bedbugs, and cockroaches.

When conditions turned hot and humid, insects infested the clothing, the sails, the food supply, and even the rigging. The sailors scratched and complained, but they had no defense against the pests. Even worse, weevils invaded the hardtack, which was further contaminated with the urine and feces of rodents. Crew members with growling stomachs forced themselves to overcome their inhibitions and swallow their disgusting, contaminated food.

Sailors found it nearly impossible to keep clean; many brought along soap and a rag for washing, but the only available water—seawater—caused itching and irritation. The sailors washed their clothes in seawater as well, with limited results.

To keep warm and dry, sailors wore baggy, loosely fitting clothes consisting of a floppy shirt, often with a hood, over which they wore a woolen pullover. Sailors were known everywhere for their pajama-like pants, which reached below the knees.

In bad weather, sailors and officers alike wore blue capes; it was a common sight to see a watchman huddled within his cape, leaving only his head exposed, peering across a storm-tossed deck for hours on end. Sailors protected their heads (and ears) with a woolen cap called a *bonete*: more than any other article of clothing, the *bonete* was the mark of a sailor.

Sailors stored their gear in large chests. The chests frequently contained a supply of playing cards—probably the most popular pastime aboard the ships of the Armada de Molucca—and books. Strict censorship laws forced sailors to submit all books they brought to sea for approval, but a few histories found their way aboard, including Marco Polo's *Travels*.

If the sailors had a moment before reporting to duty, they might relieve themselves, an unpleasant, even ridiculous chore aboard the ships. To urinate, they stood and faced the ocean wherever they could be sure that the wind would not send the stream back on them, or anyone else. Defecating was even more difficult, calling for a dangerous balancing act as a sailor eased himself over the rail and lowered himself onto a crude seat suspended high above the waves.

Weary sailors scrubbed, repaired, overhauled, and polished every exposed surface of the ships. After several months at sea, the five ships of the Armada de Molucca were in far better shape than they had been when they sailed from Seville. Nonetheless, was it any wonder that a sailor might call his ship, with all its filth and noise and nauseating odor, a *pájaro puerco* (flying pig)?

———

The men quickly left behind the identities they had maintained on land for those imposed on them at sea. A rigid division of labor ruled them all. At the bottom were the pages, assigned to the ships in pairs. Many pages were mere children, as young as eight years old, none older than fifteen. Not all pages were created equal. Some were orphans who had been virtually kidnapped from the quays of Seville and forced into service; if they had not been brought onto the ships, they would have been roaming the streets, learning to pick pockets and getting into minor scrapes. Their chores included scrubbing the decks with salt water hauled from the sea in buckets, serving meals, and cleaning up afterward.

Another class of page lived a very different life, privileged and relatively free of demand, under the protection of an officer. These handpicked young men generally came from good, well-connected families and worked as apprentices for their protectors; they were expected to learn their trade and to rise through the ranks.

The privileged pages maintained the sixteen Venetian sand clocks—or *ampolettas*—carried by Magellan's ships. Basically a large hourglass, the sand clock had been in use since Egyptian times; they were essential for both timekeeping and for navigation. Maintaining the *ampolettas* was simple enough—the pages turned them over every half hour, night and day—but the task was critical. A ship without a functioning *ampoletta* was effectively disabled.

Just above the pages in rank were the *grumetes* (apprentices). Ranging in age from seventeen to twenty, these young men were the ones who sprang on the rigging the moment the captain ordered them to furl or unfurl the sail, scampered to the dangerous lookout posts atop the masts, pulled on the oars in the longboats, and operated the complex mechanical devices aboard ship—the pulleys and cranes, the cables and anchors, the fixed and movable rigging.

If an apprentice survived the ordeals and hazards of life at sea, he could apply for certification as a "sailor," receiving a document signed by the ship's pilot, boatswain, and master. Now a professional mariner, he could look forward to a career lasting about twenty years, if he lived that long. Sailors advanced through the ranks by learning how to handle the helm; deploy the sounding line; splice cables; and, if they were mathematically inclined, mark charts and take measurements of celestial objects to locate the ship's position.

Most sailors were in their teens or twenties. Anyone who had reached his thirties was considered a veteran. Men rarely went to sea beyond the age of forty. Magellan, nearly that age when he left Seville, was among the oldest men, if not *the* oldest man, aboard the Armada de Molucca.

No matter how high an ordinary sailor rose, he was outranked by specialists such as gunners. Skilled in the use of cannon, the preparation of gunpowder, and the selection of projectiles, a gunner tended to his weapons throughout the voyage, keeping them secure, clean, free of rust, and ready for battle at all times.

Working in less glamorous but equally necessary fields of specialization were carpenters, caulkers, and coopers. This last group repaired the hundreds of casks and buckets aboard the ships by replacing hoops or staves, and sealing leaks.

Also aboard the fleet was a group of divers, whose job was to swim under the ships, clear seaweed from the rudder and keel, and inspect the hull for signs of exterior damage and leaks.

The ship's barber, another specialist, was deceptively named, because trimming beards was the least of his responsibilities. He served as the on-board dentist, doctor, and surgeon, tending to the crew out of his chest of medicines, herbs, and folk remedies. The barber's most frequent duty at sea was extracting teeth, not curing disease. The fleet's barber, Hernando de Bustamante, shipped out aboard *Concepción*.

No one answered to the description of cook aboard these ships, because the job was considered too degrading. So the crew either took turns cooking or paid the apprentices to cook for them. And during bad weather, there was no cooking at all; the sailors endured cold meals of hardtack, salted meat, and wine.

Officers ranked just above the sailors and specialists in the fleet's hierarchy. One tier consisted of the steward, who kept an eye on the food supply; the *contramaestre* (boatswain), responsible for the main body of the ship and all of the ship's equipment; the boatswain's mate; and the *alguacil*. The *alguacil* (corresponding to master-at-arms, although the term has no exact translation) served as the king's representative and military officer. If Magellan needed to arrest a crew member, he ordered the *alguacil* to perform the deed.

At the top of the labor force were the pilot, who plotted the ship's route; the master, who supervised the precious cargo; and finally the captain. Each of the top three officers had his own page (as captain general, Magellan had several pages, including his illegitimate son), and all lived lives as separate as possible from the rank-and-file sailors and apprentices.

The officers had their own cabins, cramped but a mark of distinction, and they rarely ate with the crew. To most of the men aboard the fleet—even those on the flagship, *Trinidad*—Ferdinand Magellan was a removed figure, a man whose every word was law, and on whose skill, luck, and good judgment their lives depended. In addition, a sailor was bound to go wherever the captain ordered, even "to the end of the world." So Magellan had the right to take his crew wherever he wished—all the way to the Spice Islands, and even beyond.

———

Why did sailors put up with it all? They went to sea for a variety of reasons: for glory; out of habit, desperation, or greed; and through pure chance. They went to sea because it was their livelihood, and in all likelihood their fathers' before them; because they knew the sea better than they knew land; because they could throw off the concerns of ordinary life; or because, if they stayed home, they knew the dreary routines in store for them.

Many of the men went to sea simply to escape. Some were abandoning their families and responsibilities, others were fleeing punishments such as hanging or torture, and still others were avoiding prison. Once they obtained positions on a ship, sailors were immune to arrest, safe for as long as they were at sea.

Many sailors planned to desert their ships once they reached the legendary Indies, with its gold and women and luxury. For them, the Indies served, in the words of the Spanish writer Miguel de Cervantes, as "the shelter and refuge of Spain's desperadoes, the church of the lawless, the safe haven of murderers, the native land and cover for cardsharps, the general lure for loose women, and the common deception of the many and the remedy of the particular few."

———————

In the late hours of January 10, 1520, a severe storm ravaged the Armada de Molucca, forcing Magellan to seek shelter. He ordered the fleet to reverse course and head north, toward the shelter of Paranaguá Bay. But irregular winds blew the fleet off course, and Magellan found himself in dangerously shallow waters. Before him stretched the mouth of the Río de la Plata, a funnel-shaped river located on the coast of what is now Argentina.

Magellan faced a difficult choice. If he lowered sail and tried to ride out the storm, the winds might blow his helpless fleet onto the shoals, or even ashore. But if he attempted to enter the harbor under short sail, he might run aground in the shallow water. He chose to continue north with extreme caution; he made sure to sound the waters, and learned to his relief that they were deep enough for his ships to pass unharmed.

When the storm finally ended, Magellan returned to the Río de la Plata. Many on board the fleet argued that the river led to the strait that cut across South America, although Magellan remained skeptical. A channel or a strait would be deeper, he thought, and its current would run faster. Still, he would have to conduct a careful surveillance, just in case. Unwilling to commit the entire fleet to the river, Magellan temporarily abandoned *Trinidad* to explore the waterway for himself aboard *Santiago*, the smallest ship. *Santiago* sailed upstream, constantly sounding the river, trying to avoid running aground.

The river was too shallow for the ships to pass safely, and too shallow to suggest that it was a strait running all the way to Asia and the Spice Islands. Magellan made up his mind to turn back, and once he decided on a course of action, nothing could stop him. At the end of January, he reversed direction, now facing directly into winds that made his return downriver to the coast painfully slow.

Meanwhile, even if there was no strait, the fleet had at least found abundant provisions. During the next two weeks, the men found fresh water and caught fish.

———

On February 2, 1520, the fleet resumed its southward course in search of the real strait—if it existed—but no sooner had they weighed anchor than *San Antonio* was found to be leaking badly, probably the result of having scraped the bottom in the Río de la Plata. Within two days, the leak was repaired, and the Armada de Molucca rounded what is now known as Mar del Plata.

To make sure he did not sail past the strait, Magellan dropped anchor at night and resumed sailing in the morning as close to shore as he dared, always on the lookout for any formation suggesting a strait.

Without realizing it, the sailors were heading into latitudes notorious for sudden, frequent, and violent squalls. On February 13, they ran into another powerful storm, which tossed the boats, damaged *Victoria*'s keel, and terrified the sailors with thunder, lightning, and torrential downpours. When the storm finally blew itself out, Saint Elmo's fire once again appeared on the masts of the flagship, lighting the way and reassuring the sailors that they enjoyed divine protection.

The next day, *Victoria* struck bottom not once, but several times. Colliding with a shoal was a sickening sensation dreaded by every sailor. By waiting for a rising tide, *Victoria* managed to free herself from the shoal's grip each time, but Magellan, in search of deeper water, eventually decided to lead the fleet away from shore and shoals even though he could no longer see land—or a strait.

———

The farther south he went, the more concerned Magellan became that he had accidentally passed the strait. The fate of the expedition depended on finding it. But after six months at sea, Magellan's ability to lead the armada was still in serious doubt. Many of the most influential Castilian officers, and even the Portuguese pilots, were convinced that their fierce and rigid captain general was leading them to their deaths in his search for the Spice Islands. Few among them had confidence that Magellan could lead them to the edge of the world and beyond with a reasonable chance of survival.

A crucial evolution of Magellan's style of leadership, and perhaps his character, was about to occur. The Magellan of February 1520 teetered on the brink of being murdered by the men he commanded. The Magellan of October 1520 would be on the way to earning a place in history.

CHAPTER FIVE

THE CRUCIBLE ____ OF LEADERSHIP

Finally, on February 27, the armada explored a promising inlet with two islands sheltering what appeared to be numerous ducks. Magellan named the inlet Bahía de los Patos (Duck Bay) and carefully explored it to locate an entrance to the strait.

He committed six seamen to a landing party ordered to find supplies, mainly wood for fire and fresh water. Fearful of stumbling across hostile native people in the forest, the landing party confined their activities to a tiny island lacking both fresh water and wood but full of wildlife. On closer inspection, what appeared to be ducks turned out to be something quite different. Antonio Pigafetta identified them as "geese" and "goslings." There were too many to count, he said, and wonderfully easy to catch. From his description, it is clear that the "geese" were actually penguins.

Continuing to hunt for food, the seamen crept up on a family of "sea wolves," or sea lions, stunned them with clubs, and lugged as many as they could into the longboat. Before the landing party could return to the fleet, they were stranded by a severe storm. In the morning, Magellan sent a rescue team. When they found only the abandoned longboat, the rescuers feared the worst. They carefully explored the island, calling out for their lost crewmates. Finally the rescue party found the lost men huddled beneath the lifeless sea wolves, spattered with mud, exhausted, giving off a dreadful smell, but alive. They had settled next to the creatures to find shelter from the violent storm and enough warmth to sustain them through the night.

————

As if these men had not suffered enough, another storm blasted the island just as they attempted to return to the fleet. They managed to make it back safely to the ships, but the squall was fierce enough that *Trinidad*'s mooring cables parted, one after the other. Helpless in the storm, tumbling wildly, hurling her crew this way and that, the flagship veered dangerously close to the rocks near the shore. Only one cable held, and if it gave, *Trinidad* and her men—Magellan included—would all be lost. The sailors prayed to the Virgin and to all the saints they knew. They promised to make religious pilgrimages on their return to Spain if they survived this ordeal.

Their prayers were answered when not one but three glorious instances of Saint Elmo's fire danced on the ships' yardarms, casting an unearthly light. To the religious sailors, these signs were clear evidence that God still watched over them and protected them even in the remotest regions of the globe. As proof, the sole cable protecting them from disaster held until dawn, when the storm finally relented.

Battered by the storm, Magellan sought shelter in a cove, but the weather refused to cooperate. The wind disappeared, and the Armada de Molucca remained becalmed until midnight, when it was hit by a third storm, the most destructive yet. The gale lasted three days and three nights. The fierce wind and seas tore away masts, castles, even poop decks. Through it all, the frightened sailors, trapped in disintegrating vessels that threatened to send them to their deaths at any moment, prayed for salvation with a desperate intensity.

Once again, their prayers were answered. The five ships rode out the great storm. The damage inflicted by the wind and waves, while serious, could be repaired. Incredibly, no lives were lost, despite all the hazards the sailors had encountered on land and on sea. The captain general gave the order, and the armada finally set sail.

Leaving the harbor, now named the Bay of Toil, the armada resumed its southerly course into even colder weather. With winter approaching in the southern hemisphere, Magellan had had enough of exploration; he decided to suspend the search for the strait until the following spring. He turned his attention to finding a safe harbor where the fleet could shelter from the approaching cold weather.

On March 31, he found it. From his vantage point aboard *Trinidad*, it appeared to be an ideal haven: the harbor was sheltered, and abundant fish punctured the water's surface as if in welcome. The harbor was named Port Saint Julian.

Magellan considered Port Saint Julian an important landmark. He tried to determine its longitude. He consulted Andrés de San Martín, his official astronomer. They concluded that they might have strayed into Portuguese territory, as defined by the Treaty of Tordesillas. The idea appalled Magellan, under orders from King Charles to avoid Portuguese waters.

The matter was potentially so serious, so damaging to the entire enterprise, that the pilots deliberately obscured the location of Port Saint Julian on their charts.

———

Anticipating a long, grueling winter in Port Saint Julian, Magellan placed his crew on short rations, even though the ships were filled with the butchered meat of penguins and sea lions, and fish from the harbor. Outraged by the rationing, the crew turned rebellious. Some insisted that they return to full rations, while others demanded that the fleet, or some part of it, sail back to Spain.

———

On April 1, the officers and crew observed what they, as Catholics, considered the holiest day of the year: Easter Sunday. At that moment, Magellan had one main concern: Who was loyal to him, and who was not? Magellan expected to see all four captains at Easter mass, but only one, Luis de Mendoza, of *Victoria*, arrived. The air crackled with tension. "Both conversed," the pilot Ginés de Mafra recalled, "concealing their emotions under blank countenances, and attended mass together." At the end of the ceremony, Magellan bluntly asked Mendoza why the other captains had defied his orders and failed to attend. Mendoza replied, lamely, that perhaps the others were ill.

Still pretending to be friendly, Magellan invited Mendoza to dine at the captain general's table, a gesture that would force *Victoria's* captain to state his loyalty to Magellan, but Mendoza coolly declined the request. The captain general now knew that Mendoza was a conspirator.

Mendoza returned to *Victoria*, where he and the other captains were plotting against Magellan, sending messages by longboat from one ship to another. After mass, only Magellan's first cousin, Álvaro de Mesquita, the recently appointed captain of *San Antonio*, came aboard *Trinidad* to dine at the captain general's table.

At that moment, Magellan capitalized on a piece of luck. Gaspar de Quesada's longboat, busily ferrying conspiratorial messages between the rebel ships, lost its way in the strong current and found itself drifting helplessly toward the flagship and Magellan himself, the one individual the conspirators did not want to encounter at that moment. To their surprise, the crew of *Trinidad*, at Magellan's direction, rescued them from the runaway longboat. Even more amazing, Magellan welcomed them aboard the flagship and provided them with a lavish meal, which included plenty of wine.

At dinner, the band of would-be mutineers drank a great deal and decided that they had nothing to fear from the captain general after all. They revealed the existence of the mutineers' plot, and they confided that if the plot succeeded, Magellan would be "captured and killed" that very night.

Hearing this, Magellan lost all interest in his visitors and busied himself with readying the flagship against attack. He questioned his crew to see who was loyal to him and who was not, and, satisfied that *Trinidad's* men, at least, would take his side when the mutiny erupted, awaited the assault.

———

Late that night, *Concepción* stirred with life. The captain, Quesada, lowered himself into a longboat and quietly made his way to *San Antonio*. He was joined there by Juan de Cartagena, the former captain; Juan Sebastián Elcano, a veteran Basque mariner who served as *Concepción's* master; and a corps of thirty armed seamen.

Under the cover of darkness, they boarded *San Antonio* and rushed to the captain's cabin, entering with a show of force, throwing Mesquita out of his bunk. This had once been Cartagena's ship, and in his mind, it still was. Mesquita offered little resistance as the party of mutineers clapped him into irons and led him to the cabin of the clerk, Gerónimo Guerra, where he was placed under guard.

By this time, word of the uprising had spread throughout the ship, and the crew sprang to life. Juan de Lorriage, the ship's master and a Basque, heroically tried to dismiss Quesada from *San Antonio* before any blood was shed, but Quesada refused to stand down.

"We cannot be foiled in our work by this fool," Quesada shouted, knowing that there could be no turning back. He then stabbed Lorriage with a dagger again and again, four times in all, until Lorriage, bleeding profusely, collapsed.

As the two struggled, Quesada's guard took mate Diego Hernández hostage, and suddenly the ship was without officers. The confused crew, without anyone to give them orders and fearing for their lives, gave up their arms to the mutineers. Antonio de Coca, the fleet's accountant, actually joined the mutineers, who stored the confiscated weapons in his cabin. The first phase of the mutiny had gone off as planned.

————

San Antonio was quickly converted into a battleship. Elcano, the Basque mariner, took command and immediately ordered the imprisonment of two Portuguese who appeared loyal to Magellan. The mutineers raided the ship's stores, filling their hungry bellies with bread and wine, anything they could lay their hands on.

The armada's chaplain, Pedro de Valderrama, preoccupied with administering last rites to Lorriage, watched all and vowed to report the evil deeds to Magellan, if he ever got the chance. Meanwhile, Elcano ordered firearms be prepared.

Within hours the mutiny spread to two other ships: *Victoria*, whose captain, Luis de Mendoza, had resented Magellan from the day they left Sanlúcar de Barrameda, and *Concepción*. It was a matter of time until Cartagena, Quesada, and their supporters came after Magellan himself. Only *Santiago*, under the command of Juan Rodríguez Serrano, a Castilian, remained neutral. Quesada, for the moment, decided to leave *Santiago* alone; it was a decision that would later haunt the mutineers.

———————

The sun rose over Port Saint Julian on April 2 to reveal a scene of false calm. The five ships of the Armada de Molucca rode quietly at anchor. For the moment, the captain general remained secure in *Trinidad*. As a test of loyalty, he dispatched a longboat to *San Antonio* to bring sailors ashore to fetch fresh water. As *Trinidad*'s longboat approached, the mutineers waved the sailors away and declared that *San Antonio* was no longer under the command of Mesquita or Magellan. She now belonged to the mutineer Gaspar de Quesada.

When the longboat brought this disturbing news back to Magellan, he realized he faced a serious problem. He sent the longboat to poll the other ships and determine their loyalty. From *San Antonio*, Quesada replied, "For the King and for myself," and *Victoria* and *Concepción* followed suit.

To make his point, Quesada boldly sent a list of demands to the flagship. Quesada believed, with good reason, that he had Magellan boxed in, and he tried to force the captain general to yield to the mutineers. In writing, Quesada declared that he was now in charge of the fleet, and he intended to end the harsh treatment Magellan had inflicted on the officers and crew. Quesada promised that he would feed them better, would not endanger their lives, and would return to

Spain. If Magellan agreed to these demands, said Quesada, the mutineers would yield control of the armada to him.

To Magellan, these demands were outrageous. To comply meant humiliation in Spain, disgrace in Portugal, years in a prison cell, or even death. But Magellan sent back word that he would be pleased to hear the mutineers out—aboard the flagship, of course. The mutineers were hesitant to leave their base. Who knew what awaited them aboard *Trinidad*? They replied that they would meet him only aboard *San Antonio*. To their astonishment, Magellan agreed.

———————

Having lulled Quesada and his followers into a sense of security, Magellan quietly went on the offensive.

He began his attempt to recover his fleet by capturing the longboat carrying Quesada's communiqué. With this piece of equipment in hand, he turned his attention to recapturing at least one ship, and once that was in his camp he would go after the others. He decided to attempt to reclaim not *San Antonio*, where the mutineers were deeply committed, but rather *Victoria*, where support for the rebels might be softer and where he would be most likely to find support.

Victoria became the key to the whole plan, and to get it back, Magellan resorted to a con. He filled the captured longboat with five carefully selected sailors and instructed them to appear sympathetic to the mutineers, at least at a distance. But beneath their loose clothing they carried weapons. Their ranks included Gonzalo Gómez de Espinosa, the *alguacil*.

Magellan gave the men a letter addressed to Luis de Mendoza, *Victoria*'s captain, ordering him to surrender immediately aboard the flagship. If Mendoza resisted, they were to kill him.

As soon as the longboat moved out of sight to begin its mission, the captain general sent a second skiff into the water, filled with fifteen loyal members of the flagship's crew under the command of Duarte Barbosa, Magellan's brother-in-law.

When the first longboat pulled up to *Victoria*, Mendoza allowed the party to board his ship. According to other witnesses, Mendoza responded to Magellan's letter with laughter, crumpled the orders into a ball, and carelessly tossed it overboard. At that, Espinosa, the military officer, grabbed Mendoza by the beard and stabbed him. *Victoria's* captain slumped to the deck, lifeless.

With Mendoza dead, Magellan held the advantage in the life-and-death contest. No sooner had the captain breathed his last breath than the second longboat rowed into position beside *Victoria*, discharging loyalists, who stormed the ship. As Magellan had calculated, there was little or no opposition. Stunned by the death of their captain, the crew meekly submitted to Magellan's men.

As if the sight of the dead officer was not insult enough to the other Castilians, Magellan later paid off Espinosa and his henchmen for this bloody deed in plain view of everyone. Was this the price of their lives? A few ducats?

————

To signal Magellan's triumph, Barbosa flew the captain general's colors from *Victoria's* mast, announcing to Quesada and the other rebels that the mutiny was ending. Magellan placed *Trinidad* securely between the two loyal ships, *Victoria* guarding one side and *Santiago*, now loyal to Magellan, the other. Together, the three vessels blockaded the inlet to the port; the two rebel holdouts, positioned deeper in the harbor, could not escape.

Magellan expected Quesada to recognize that resistance was pointless. The mutiny had failed, and the mutineer would soon have to bargain not for better rations or a swift return to Spain, but for his very life. Still, Quesada refused to give up.

Concepción and *San Antonio* remained at the other end of the harbor. To prevent them from slipping past the blockade at night, Magellan readied his flagship for combat. He doubled the watch and warned the guards not to let the two rebellious ships escape from the harbor into the open sea.

While the others were distracted, Magellan secretly gave a seaman a dangerous assignment. Under cover of darkness, he was to sneak on board Quesada's ship, *Concepción*, where he would cut the anchor cable so that she would slip her mooring. Magellan calculated that the strong nocturnal ebb tide would draw her toward the blockade guarding the mouth of the harbor, giving him just the excuse he needed for launching a surprise attack. He was prepared to greet her with all the firepower he could muster.

Late that night, *Concepción* drifted mysteriously across the harbor. Because no one knew Magellan's strategy, she appeared to be dragging her anchor. It was only a matter of time until she came within range of the flagship.

The rebellion was beginning to weaken. Quesada, the leader of the mutiny, was experiencing pangs of regret, but he could not persuade his followers to end their rebellion now.

As *Concepción* approached the flagship, Magellan shouted, "Treason! Treason!" and ordered his men to ready their weapons.

Suddenly, *Trinidad* opened fire on the approaching vessel, the massive *lombardas* (a type of cannon) hurling cannonballs onto her decks. Before Quesada's men could fight back, *Trinidad*'s loyal seamen grappled *Concepción* to her side and rushed aboard as *Victoria* performed the same maneuver on the hapless ship's starboard side.

"Who are you for?" the attackers cried as they swarmed across *Concepción*'s cramped decks.

"For the king," came the response, "and Magellan!"

The mutineers' about-face may have saved their lives, because Magellan's guard made straight for Quesada and his inner circle, who offered little resistance. The guard freed Mesquita, the overthrown captain (and Magellan's first cousin), along with the pilot, Ginés de Mafra.

With Quesada and his inner circle under arrest, and *Concepción* returned to Magellan's control, the midnight mutiny of Port Saint Julian came to an embarrassing conclusion. Juan de Cartagena, aboard

San Antonio, gave up hope of carrying out a mutiny. When the flagship drew alongside *San Antonio*, and Magellan demanded Cartagena's immediate surrender, the rebellious Castilian timidly obeyed and was confined in irons in *Trinidad's* hold.

That morning, the captain general had controlled just one ship; now he ruled all five.

Now that the Easter Mutiny was finally at an end, Magellan handed out punishment to the guilty parties. To begin, the captain general ordered his men to tear Mendoza's lifeless body to pieces. More than execution, such a display of barbarism was his ultimate weapon at sea. That he resorted to harsh physical punishment, including torture, was not unusual; this was, after all, the era of the Spanish Inquisition (the brutal court system used by the Catholic Church in Spain to root out heretics).

Through Magellan's use of torture, his crew came to understand that the only thing worse than obeying Magellan and possibly losing their lives in the process, was suffering the consequences of defying him. One of the reasons his crew had the courage and determination to circumnavigate the globe, even if it meant sailing over the edge of the world, was that he forced them to do so. Fear was his most important means of motivating his men; they became more afraid of Magellan than of the hazards of the sea.

To punish the other offenders, Magellan conducted an inquisition at Port Saint Julian. He appointed his cousin Álvaro de Mesquita as judge presiding over an exhaustive trial. First Magellan had promoted Mesquita to captain of the *San Antonio* over the heads of more qualified pilots and master seamen, both Spanish and Portuguese. Now Mesquita functioned as Magellan's agent of agony, deciding who was guilty of treason and who would suffer the consequences. No wonder the men hated Mesquita.

Magellan subjected at least one of the participants in the Port Saint Julian mutiny to strappado, a form of torture illustrated here by early sixteenth-century artist Domenico Beccafumi.

Mesquita spent two weeks assessing the "evidence" of guilt before passing judgment. At the end of the trial, Mesquita let one of the accused off with a slap on the wrist: the accountant Antonio de Coca was merely deprived of his rank. But Mesquita found Andrés de San Martín, the esteemed astronomer; Hernando Morales, a pilot; and a priest all guilty of treason. Mesquita ordered San Martín to undergo gruesome torture. Amazingly, San Martín survived the ordeal. The other accused—in all, forty men—were sentenced to death.

A mass execution appeared to be in the making, but the expedition could not continue without the help of the convicted men. Believing that he had finally demonstrated his absolute authority, Magellan changed all forty of the death sentences to hard labor.

Desertion was impossible; no one could survive the harsh climate. The only choice left was a slavish obedience to Magellan's authority, even if that authority led the armada over the edge of the world.

———

There were two important exceptions to the general forgiveness: Gaspar de Quesada, the leader and murderer of *San Antonio*'s master, and Quesada's servant, Luis de Molino. Magellan insisted that Quesada be executed. And he gave Molino a brutally simple choice: he could either be executed along with his master or spare his own life by beheading his master. As Magellan expected, Molino accepted the deal, as cruel as it was, and chose to live.

———

Days later, Magellan discovered that Cartagena, the sole surviving Spanish captain, was conspiring with a priest, Pero Sánchez de la Reina, to mount yet another mutiny.

The captain general subjected the two conspirators to a fresh court-martial. His first instinct was to have both men executed—this was, after all, Cartagena's third attempt at mutiny—but Magellan found himself in a difficult position. He could not bring himself to condemn a priest, even a disloyal priest, to death. And as for Cartagena, his blood ties to Archbishop Fonseca prevented Magellan from taking severe disciplinary action such as execution or torture. Instead, Magellan decided to leave the two men behind to fend for themselves in the wilderness of Port Saint Julian after the fleet's departure.

———

Always a perfectionist about outfitting his ships, Magellan turned his attention to his neglected fleet. The ships were in a state of disrepair, their sails and rigging in disarray, their holds rotting, their hulls leaky. He ordered his men to empty the ships and give them a thorough cleaning. The forty mutineers, bound in chains, performed the most grueling labor; they operated the pumps, an essential chore for keeping the ships afloat until the armada's carpenters made them seaworthy again. Overseeing these projects, Magellan would keep his prisoners in chains until they left Port Saint Julian in the spring.

When the time came to load the provisions, they discovered that the dishonest chandlers in Seville and the Canary Islands had robbed them blind and thus endangered their lives. Magellan realized the ships would likely run out of food well before they reached their goal. The men resumed hunting to make up the difference, but they were eating their way through their supplies almost as fast they replenished them. The only way out of their predicament was to resume the voyage as soon as possible, storms or no storms.

CHAPTER SIX
CASTAWAYS

In late April 1520, Magellan rashly sent out a reconnaissance mission to search for the elusive strait that he believed would lead him to the Spice Islands. He selected *Santiago*, the soundest of the vessels, for the task, with Juan Rodríguez Serrano as her captain. Serrano was about to meet the ultimate challenge of his career.

Even if Serrano found the mouth of the strait, he would have to survive an equally dangerous return journey to Port Saint Julian. And the temptation to mutiny and sail away—either east toward Spain or west through the strait—might be irresistible to *Santiago*'s crew.

Magellan quieted thoughts of escape by keeping the provisions on board *Santiago* to a minimum and offering Serrano a reward of one hundred ducats if the expedition located the strait; of course, Serrano could collect only on his return.

Favored by calm weather, the mission began auspiciously enough. On May 3, about sixty miles south of Port Saint Julian, Serrano discovered an inlet that, on closer inspection, revealed itself as the mouth of a river, which he named Santa Cruz.

Santiago's crew soon discovered that food was even more plentiful around the Santa Cruz River than at Port Saint Julian, and Serrano decided to linger for six days to fish and hunt for elephant seals.

After the tranquil break, *Santiago* set sail and proceeded south in search of the strait. On May 22, the wind picked up and the seas began to churn. The armada had encountered many violent squalls, but little *Santiago* had stumbled into the most powerful storm her crew had ever experienced, and they would have to face it alone.

Serrano had no time to reef the sails. Fierce seas pounded the ship mercilessly, terrifying her crew. Serrano attempted to head into the wind and ride out the storm, but overpowering gusts tore the sails, and the seas battered the rudder until it failed to respond. *Santiago* was now out of control, caught in the middle of a storm that was still building in power, her men beyond the hope of rescue. As the storm gathered force and the winds pushed the helpless ship toward the rocky coast and the prospect of certain death, Serrano faced every captain's nightmare. Razor-sharp rocks sawed into the ship's hull, and she began taking on water.

But luck was with her crew, as *Santiago* washed ashore before breaking up. One by one, the thirty-seven crewmen crawled to the end of the jib boom and jumped to a rocky beach. As soon as they had abandoned ship, *Santiago* broke up and the storm carried away all her life-sustaining provisions—wine, hardtack, and water.

Incredibly, all the men aboard the ship had survived, but the storm had stranded the castaways seventy miles from the rest of the fleet, without food or wood or fresh water, in freezing weather. They were cold and exhausted; soon they would be starving. There was no way to get word to the captain general. Their land route back to Port Saint Julian presented seemingly overwhelming obstacles: snow-covered mountains and the Santa Cruz River, three miles wide.

———————

The castaways spent eight days in more or less the same area, disoriented, waiting for pieces of the wreck, possibly even food, to drift onto the beach, but the sea yielded only a few broken planks from *Santiago*'s hull. Surviving on a diet of local vegetation and whatever shellfish they could catch, the castaways evolved a plan. They would drag the planks with them over the mountains until they reached the river, and there, on its banks, build a raft to cross it. The river was only a few miles to the north, but the task of carrying and dragging the planks over the mountains to its shores turned out to be too much for the crew. They left most of the planks behind, and after four wretched days of marching overland, the exhausted crew finally reached the broad expanse of the river. The weather had calmed, and fish, as they knew from their first visit to the river, were plentiful. It seemed they would not starve after all.

Lacking planks to build a raft large enough to carry all the men, the castaways split into two groups. The larger group—thirty-five men—set up camp at the river's edge, while two strong men, whose names were not recorded, set out on the tiny raft they had managed to build. They intended to cross the river and walk the rest of the way back to Port Saint Julian to seek help. It was an exceedingly risky plan. Successfully crossing the three-mile expanse of river required a combination of bravery and luck, and when they reached the other side, they would face a grueling march in freezing weather, living off the land.

The two crew members made it across the river in their basic raft, and once they had landed on the far side, they set out in the direction of Port Saint Julian. The trek lasted eleven tormenting days, and when they reached Port Saint Julian, ravaged and emaciated from their ordeal, even those who knew the survivors barely recognized them.

Once the castaways revived, they described the desperate situation of their shipmates on the far side of the Santa Cruz River.

———

Magellan had no choice but to attempt to rescue the other thirty-five crew members of *Santiago*. Afraid to risk the loss of another ship to a storm, he sent a rescue squad of twenty-four men, carrying wine and hardtack, along the overland trail that the two survivors had blazed through the harsh wilderness. Finally, weakened from their days in the wild, they reached the exhausted castaways, who had been camping out along the banks of the Santa Cruz River. Relying on the small raft cobbled together from the wreck of *Santiago*, the rescue party ferried the survivors back across the river in groups of two or at most three; miraculously, everyone made it to the northern shore.

As Magellan anxiously awaited the outcome of the rescue mission, the thirty-five castaways and twenty-four rescuers picked their way through the snows of the Patagonian winter. About a week later, they emerged from the forest surrounding Port Saint Julian. Driven by an unshakable will to survive, everyone made it back safely.

Magellan greeted the dazed, exhausted men with lots of food and wine, and treated them all as heroes.

––––––––

The wreck of *Santiago* and the hardship endured by her crew troubled Magellan more deeply than the violence and torture of the Easter Mutiny. The disaster confirmed his crew's fear that the captain general was leading them on an expedition so dangerous that they would all get killed long before they reached the Spice Islands.

To ensure his control of the remaining four ships in the fleet, he saw to it that only diehard loyalists commanded them. While Álvaro de Mesquita, his first cousin, remained in command of *San Antonio*, Magellan appointed Duarte Barbosa, his brother-in-law, as captain of *Victoria*, and Juan Rodríguez Serrano, the unlucky skipper of *Santiago*, as the new captain of *Concepción*. Magellan himself still ruled over all from *Trinidad*. Finally, he scattered *Santiago*'s long-suffering crew among the four remaining ships to prevent them from secretly conspiring. He now had full charge of the Armada de Molucca, and was the unquestioned commander of the remaining four ships—or so he hoped.

––––––––

After the loss of *Santiago*, Magellan was determined to wait for spring before he resumed searching for the strait. In the midst of the empty winter months, Magellan and the rest of his fleet were distracted by an unexpected sight: a distant plume of smoke wafting over the landscape. Perhaps they were not alone after all.

"We remained two whole months without ever seeing anyone," wrote Pigafetta of their stay in Port Saint Julian. "But one day (without anyone expecting it) we saw a giant who was on the shore, quite naked, and who danced, leaped, and sang, while he sang he threw sand and dust on his head. . . . Our captain sent one of his men toward him, charging him to leap and sing like the other to reassure him and show him friendship. Which he did."

The strange ritual recommended by Magellan worked; after

watching the European seaman imitate his gestures, the giant appeared peaceful and eager to socialize, and the dancing continued.

The Europeans marveled at the giant's stature. "He was so tall that the tallest of us only came up to his waist," the official chronicler observed. "He had a very large face, painted round with red, and his eyes also were painted round with yellow, and in the middle of his cheeks he had two hearts painted. He had hardly any hairs on his head, and was painted white."

The giant was a member of the tribe known as the Tehuelche Indians. In reality, the Tehuelche measured about six feet tall; the impression of the Indian's stature came in part from his costume and especially the elaborate boots he wore, which added to his height.

———————

Emboldened by the first encounter, Magellan invited the giant on board the flagship, where he offered his guest plentiful "food and drink." When the feast ended, a guard of four armed men escorted him to shore.

During the feast, another giant had watched the proceedings from land, and as soon as his tribesman returned safely, he sprinted off in the direction of their hidden huts to relay the news. Slowly, the other giants emerged from the trees to reveal themselves to the crew members, who were amazed by the sight of giant women.

Eventually Magellan gave the Indians a name: Pathagoni, an expression suggesting the Spanish word *patacones* (dogs with great paws), by which he meant to call attention to their big feet, made even larger by the rough-hewn boots they wore. Later Magellan gave the name to the whole region, known ever since as Patagonia.

———————

On July 28, four Patagonian giants, two men and two boys, appeared at the water's edge, signaling to the fleet that they wished to come aboard. This was just the opportunity Magellan had been waiting for. A longboat was dispatched to bring the four unsuspecting Indians aboard *Trinidad*. Magellan gave presents to his guests—"knives, scissors, mirrors, bells, and glass"—and while the four held them and marveled at them, "the captain sent for large iron fetters, such as are put on the feet of malefactors." Two of the giants were shackled. Even Pigafetta was taken aback, remarking that Magellan had resorted to a "cunning trick."

Confusion overwhelmed both parties. Magellan then underwent a sudden change of heart and decided against imprisoning the giants. He ordered a detachment of nine guards under the command of João Lopes Carvalho, *Concepción*'s pilot, to escort two of the giants ashore. As soon as his feet touched dry land, one giant managed to escape. Carvalho feared that he would tell others about the trick played on the giants and that the tribe would return, seeking retaliation.

That night, Carvalho decided they would sleep ashore. In the morning, the Indians' intentions became clear when arrows began whizzing from the dark forest. Suddenly, nine Indian warriors appeared. Each carried three quivers of arrows suspended from a leather girdle around his waist, one in front, and one on either side. With fluid movements, the warriors fired off one deadly arrow after another. "Fighting thus, one of these giants pierced one of our men in the thigh, who died immediately. Whereupon seeing him dead they all fled."

Furious, the other crew members retaliated with all their might. Their muskets' deafening roar scattered the giants, and when quiet returned to Port Saint Julian, the crew sorrowfully buried their fallen colleague.

Magellan still held two Indians hostage, one aboard *Trinidad*, the other assigned to *San Antonio*, and despite the ban on passengers, slaves, or stowaways, he intended to present these two giants to King Charles.

———

On August 11, 1520, two weeks before the fleet would leave Port Saint Julian, Magellan carried out the sentence for his nemesis, Juan de Cartagena, and the priest, Pero Sánchez de la Reina, who had conspired with the Castilian captain. At Magellan's order, both were marooned on a small island in sight of the ships. They had no longboat, no firewood, and very little clothing. Their supplies consisted mainly of hardtack and wine, enough to last them the summer, perhaps, but they would have to face the next winter in Port Saint Julian alone.

Magellan finally gave the command to weigh anchor on August 24. After the five-month layover in Port Saint Julian, the Armada de Molucca put to sea. As the four ships sailed into the open waters of the Atlantic, the abandoned conspirators, Cartagena and the priest, kneeled at the water's edge, crying and pleading for mercy as the ships grew smaller and finally vanished over the horizon.

The strait still eluded the fleet, but, God willing, they would find it, reach the Spice Islands, and eventually return to Spain, where they would be rich enough to spend the rest of their lives in retirement. It was a fantastic dream, and their only hope of deliverance.

CHAPTER SEVEN

DRAGON'S TAIL

From the moment of their departure from Port Saint Julian, their journey southward was filled with more difficulty. After two days at sea, as they approached the mouth of the Santa Cruz River, another storm overwhelmed them and threatened to drive them all ashore, where they would likely meet the same fate as the unlucky *Santiago*. Magellan gave the order to enter the broad river, and there, sheltered from the worst of the winds, the fleet rode out the squall.

After the storm passed, Magellan, with every fiber of his being, wanted to resume the search for the strait. Yet the hazards of exploring the coast in August, as winter relented, remained overwhelming even to Magellan, who was normally fearless. With the greatest reluctance, he decided to remain at the river until well into the subequatorial spring; then, and only then, would his ships have any chance of surviving at sea.

Magellan made the most of this necessary layover. For the next six weeks, the seamen busied themselves catching fish, drying and salting them, and stocking the ships. They ventured on land only to chop wood and haul it back to the ships. Occasionally, they made brief excursions to the southern shore of the Santa Cruz, where *Santiago* had broken up, and salvaged whatever items the sea had thrown on shore, mainly chests and barrels.

On October 18, 1520, Magellan decided to risk the open sea again. He was months behind schedule—he had expected to be approaching the Spice Islands by now—and he yearned to make up for lost time. The fleet departed from the Santa Cruz River, tracing the undulating eastern coast of South America, with the captain general in the grip of his obsession to find the strait.

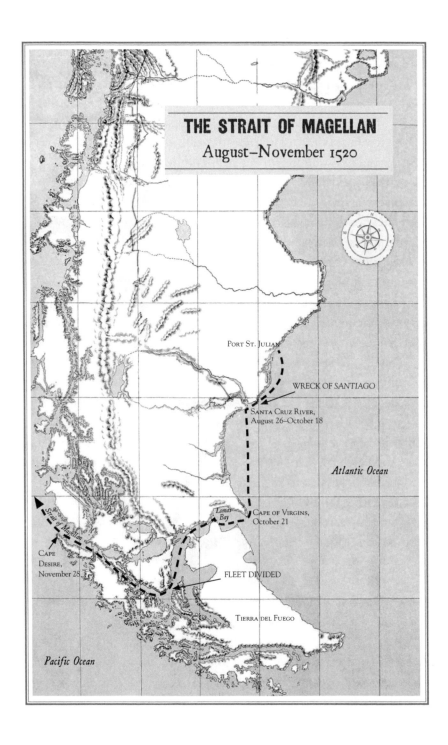

THE STRAIT OF MAGELLAN
August–November 1520

PORT ST. JULIAN

WRECK OF SANTIAGO

SANTA CRUZ RIVER,
August 26–October 18

Atlantic Ocean

Lomas
Bay

CAPE OF VIRGINS,
October 21

Strait of Magellan

CAPE
DESIRE,
November 28

FLEET DIVIDED

TIERRA DEL FUEGO

Pacific Ocean

Once again, the ships battled storms. After two difficult days without any progress, the direction of the wind changed; now it came from the north, and the four ships plunged before it, leaving sharp, bubbling wakes and making rapid progress along a south-by-southwest course. Magellan scrutinized every inlet, hoping it might contain a hidden channel leading inland, but in each instance he was disappointed and continued his southerly course. Finally, he noticed a significant spit of land extending into open waters: a cape. As he approached, he made out a broad sandbank covered with the skeletons of whales—a suggestion that he had come across a migration route, perhaps leading from the Atlantic to the Pacific.

Magellan ordered his ships to sail into the bay, and then he saw it: an outlet leading west, just as he had prayed there would be. There was no mistaking it for a bay or an inlet; a broad waterway cut deep into the dense landmass. After two bitter mutinies and weeks of hazardous, unpredictable voyaging, Magellan had finally found his strait.

———

Now Magellan faced three hundred miles of nautical nightmare. Navigating the waterway would prove as demanding a challenge as simply finding it had been. Tides in the strait ran deep, and currents were strong. Beds of kelp lurking below the water's surface frequently damaged lines, keels, and rudders. But if Magellan could overcome the obstacles presented by the strait, and keep his mutinous crew intact, he would pioneer a new route to the Indies, a new understanding of the continents, and a new conception of the globe itself.

———

As the armada negotiated the strait's frigid waters, thickly vegetated shores slid past, cloaked in eerie shadows. Late one night, during the few hours of darkness at that time of year, the sailors caught glimpses of what they believed were signs of human settlements. Distant fires with indistinct sources sent plumes of smoke into the hazy sky, polluting the air with a strong odor.

Magellan and his crew believed these fires had been set by humans who lurked in the shadows, waiting to pounce—one more reason for the sailors to stay aboard ship, especially at night, even though their provisions were running low. This was a reasonable precaution, but the fires were most likely of natural origin, the result of lightning. In any event, Magellan called this region Tierra del Fuego (Land of Fire).

Now that they were in the strait, the pilots found that the sky was rarely clear by day or night, which made it nearly impossible to take accurate measurements either by the stars or by the sun.

Although Magellan traveled through the strait at the warmest time of year, enormous glaciers surrounding the ships were plentiful and awe-inspiring: solid walls of ice rising two hundred feet, five hundred feet, higher even than the condors circling in the rising air currents overhead. They were ancient edifices, these glaciers, some of them ten thousand years old. Snow nearly always fell atop them—they were endlessly renewing themselves—and at lower altitudes the ice began to melt into narrow waterfalls that cascaded over the granite ledges into the fjords.

The glaciers were neither white nor gray, but a light, almost iridescent blue that in the crevasses and seams of the ice walls darkened to a deep azure. Countless chunks of ice broke off from the glaciers, some as large as a whale, others as small as a penguin: an armada of sculptured ice drifting toward a mysterious location.

———

Once the armada had negotiated the first two narrows within the strait, Magellan became increasingly cautious about the hazards ahead and decided to scout the strait's uncharted waters. Magellan dispatched two ships, *Concepción* and *San Antonio*, but *San Antonio* would take most of the risks.

Meanwhile, *Victoria* and *Trinidad* remained tied up in Lomas Bay, on the southerly shore of the strait. Here the water was shallow enough to permit the ships to drop anchor, and they seemed to be safe, but at night a great wind known as a williwaw blew up and lasted well into the next day, battering the ships. A williwaw in this part of the world occurs when air, chilled by the glaciers surrounding the strait, becomes unstable and suddenly races down the mountains with ever-increasing velocity. By the time it reaches the fjords, it creates a squall so powerful that it never fails to terrify and disorient any sailor unlucky enough to be caught in its grip. Magellan was forced to raise anchor and let the two ships ride out the storm in the protected reaches of the bay.

Compared with the ships that stayed behind, *San Antonio* and *Concepción* had an even more difficult time riding out the williwaw. The fierce winds prevented them from rounding the cape, and when they tried to rejoin the fleet, they nearly ran aground.

In the darkness, the two ships became disoriented, and their pilots, without maps and unable to see the stars, feared they were lost. They hunted through the next day, and the next after that, until they finally approached a narrow channel leading to a continuation of the strait. Once they noted the exact location of the strait's extension, they sailed back through relatively calm waters to find their captain general.

A dramatic reunion occurred. The rejoicing at the triumph over weather and geography and the feeling of being blessed by divine authority were new to Magellan's men. For the better part of two years, they had been deeply mistrustful of their captain general, divided by language and culture, and prone to mutiny. After passing through these ordeals, they had become united and saw in each other the possibility of ultimate triumph.

———

The strait largely consisted of a network of fjords, narrow passages that reached depths of fifteen hundred feet, and on either side snow-capped granite cliffs rose hundreds of feet. If one of Magellan's men fell overboard, he would survive in these conditions for ten minutes at the most.

Here and there, along stony gray beaches, lounged families of elephant seals. Other indigenous wildlife in the strait included arctic foxes and penguins crowding beaches of their own. Giant black-and-white condors circled overhead, their wingspan extending to ten feet.

Despite the snow cover, the waterfall-fed vegetation in the strait was suffocatingly lush. Within several feet of the shoreline lurked a dense forest with dozens of types of ferns; stunted, windblown trees; silky moss; and a layer of spongy tundra. There were also brightly colored clumps of tiny, hardy berries; they were bitter on the outside but sweet on the inside, their delicate fruit covered with miniature air cushions to protect them from snow. (The crew had to be careful about eating them; although the berries were not toxic, they had a severe laxative effect.) There were even small white orchids blooming in the mud.

The strait's thick vegetation gave the air an intoxicating fragrance. The breezes carried a damp, mossy odor lightened by the scent of wildflowers, freshened by the cool glaciers, and faintly tangy with the salt from the sea. Like everything else in this region, the very air was alive with mystery and promise.

Since leaving Port Saint Julian, Magellan had seen no indigenous peoples, but his men remained alert, both for self-protection and the opportunity to barter for provisions. He dispatched a skiff crowded with ten men under orders to comb the landscape for signs of human life, but they found only a primitive structure sheltering two hundred gravesites.

As the fleet glided along the fjords, the sailors experienced only three hours of night, and the extended days allowed them to make up for the time lost in Port Saint Julian. The prospect of successfully negotiating the strait appeared increasingly likely, at least to Magellan. Encouraged, the captains and pilots indicated they were strongly in favor of pushing on—all but one, that is.

Estêvão Gomes, the pilot of *San Antonio*, strongly disagreed. Now that they had found the strait, he argued, they should sail back to

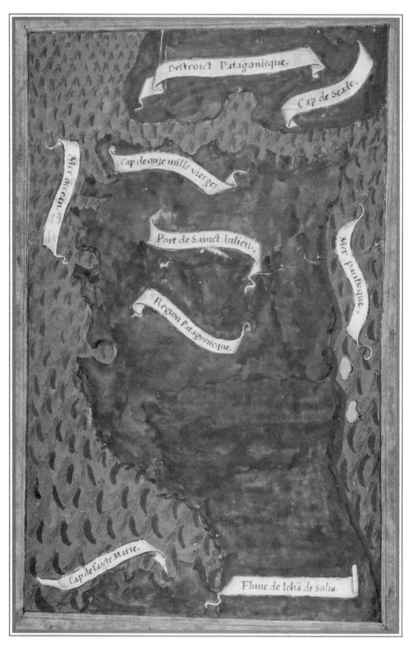

The Strait of Magellan as depicted in an edition of Antonio Pigafetta's journal from the voyage, printed in France shortly after his return to Europe. The Strait and the southern tip of Patagonia are at the top, and the Pacific Ocean is to the right.

Spain to assemble a better-equipped fleet. He reminded Magellan that they still had to cross the Pacific, and while no one knew how large it was, Gomes assumed it was a large gulf in which they might encounter disastrous storms.

Magellan considered Gomes's proposal an outrage. The captain general insisted the armada would continue at all costs, even if the men were reduced to eating the leather wrapping their masts. Not everyone shared Magellan's passionate determination. With his widely acknowledged piloting skills, Gomes had supporters among the crew, a situation that infuriated the captain general.

Gomes's opposition set the stage for another mutiny, but unlike the previous uprisings, this was not a violent confrontation with flashing swords. It began more subtly, as a grim debate at the end of the world between two respected Portuguese rivals.

———

Under Magellan's command, *Trinidad* continued the westward exploration of the strait. On October 28, little more than a week after discovering the strait, the crew tied up at an island guarding the entrance to another bay. Here the strait extended in two directions. To choose a course, Magellan dispatched two ships to investigate, giving them four days to return with their reports.

After a few days, *Victoria* returned with news, a sighting of the open ocean. Sighting the Pacific was a momentous event, but the excitement of this discovery was overshadowed by the mysterious failure of *San Antonio* to reappear at the appointed time and place. Magellan had no idea what had become of her. Perhaps she lay at the bottom of one of the fjords. Or perhaps she had deserted just when the expedition was on the verge of its great accomplishment.

San Antonio had indeed sailed for Spain, and its captain, Álvaro de Mesquita, Magellan's cousin, had been taken prisoner. The long-frustrated mutiny had finally succeeded; even worse, it had taken place when Magellan least expected it. *San Antonio* and all her crew had vanished.

Aboard the renegade *San Antonio*, the situation was more complicated than Magellan could have known. Mesquita, the captain, had attempted to rendezvous with the rest of the fleet, but he failed to locate the other ships in the strait's confusing network of estuaries. Gomes offered little help in the situation. Mesquita sent smoke signals and fired cannon to try to raise the rest of the fleet, but these signs went unseen and unheard. Mesquita insisted on continuing his search for Magellan, but the growing uncertainty convinced Gomes and a few like-minded sailors that the time had come to seize the ship. They swiftly overpowered Mesquita. Once the mutiny was in progress, there was no stopping it; the mutineers had to succeed or, as they well knew, they would be tortured and killed.

Desperate, Gomes stabbed Mesquita in the leg. Battling the wound's throbbing pain, Mesquita snatched the dagger from Gomes and stabbed the attacker in the hand. Gomes howled as the iron entered his flesh, and his cries attracted reinforcements, who overwhelmed Mesquita, shackled him, and imprisoned him in the clerk Gerónimo Guerra's cabin. Now Mesquita would receive bitter payback for the court-martial and suffering he had overseen in Port Saint Julian. As *San Antonio* set a course for Spain, the mutineers planned to torture him into signing a confession saying that Magellan had tortured Spanish officers.

San Antonio was the largest ship in the armada, and she carried many of the fleet's provisions in her hold, so the loss instantly put the other sailors' food supplies—indeed, their lives—in jeopardy. The rebels also carried off another prize, the friendly Patagonian giant whom they had captured several months before.

Magellan elected to launch a search mission to recapture the missing ship, a virtual impossibility in this watery labyrinth. When it was not found, he followed his royal instructions to establish prominent signs for lost ships. The chronicler Antonio Pigafetta wrote, "Two banners were planted with their letters—one on a little eminence in the first bay, and the other in an islet in the third bay, where there were many sea wolves and large birds." But they were lonely signals left at the end of the world for a phantom ship.

————————

Giving in to a rare moment of self-doubt, Magellan sought the advice of his remaining captains on whether to proceed with the expedition or return to Spain. Rather than summon them, Magellan dictated a lengthy letter to each officer, an indication that he feared another rebellion. The document stressed his urgent need to build a consensus. "I am aware of your deeming it a very grievous thing that I shall be determined to continue onwards, because you think that time is short to accomplish our journey," he said.

> And since I am a man who never despised the advice and opinion from others, on the contrary, all of my decisions are taken jointly with everyone and notified to one and all, without my offending anyone; and because of what happened in San Julian with the deaths of Luis de Mendoza and Gaspar de Quesada, and the banishment of Juan de Cartagena and Pero Sánchez de la Reina, priest, you out of fear refrain from telling me and advising me on everything you believe to be useful to His Majesty and the Armada's well-being, but if you do not tell me so, you are going against the service of the Emperor-King, our lord, and against the oath and homage you took with me; therefore I ask you on behalf of the said lord, and I myself beg you and order you to write down your opinions, each one individually, stating the reasons why we should continue onwards or else turn back, and all this showing no respect for anything that may prevent you from telling the truth. . . . Being aware of those reasons and opinions, I will then say mine and my willingness to conclude what should be done.
>
> —Written in the Canal of Todos los Santos, opposite the Río de la Isleta, on the 21st of November, Thursday, at fifty-three degrees, of 1520. Ordered by Captain General Ferdinand Magellan.

In this remarkable document—Magellan's longest statement to have survived—the normally resolute Magellan sounds as though he is about to apologize for the long-drawn-out trial and cruel executions he ordered at Port Saint Julian.

———————

Thrust into a position of authority, Andrés de San Martín, the fleet's astronomer, responded that they should continue the expedition at least through mid-January, although he remained skeptical that the strait would ultimately prove to be the miraculous passage to the Moluccas—the Spice Islands. After January, he warned, the days would grow short, and the williwaws would become even more ferocious. If they had not reached their goal by then, they should return to Spain and try again later. San Martín reminded Magellan that their drastically reduced provisions would not last them all the way to the Moluccas. He dared to express what nearly everyone on the voyage whispered: there was great danger ahead, and chances were they would not make it.

Magellan considered his cosmographer's carefully thought-out advice, but he instead decided to proceed, no matter how long it took to reach the Spice Islands. The armada had at least three months' provisions, by his estimation. More important, he believed that God would assist them in achieving their goal.

The next day, Magellan gave the order to weigh anchor. The ships fired a salvo of cannon that reverberated among the splendid dark green mountains, gray ravines, and azure glaciers of the strait, and the armada set sail once again, heading west, always west.

At last, the churning Pacific came into view. Magellan had done it; he had found the waterway, just as he had promised King Charles. Now that the armada had accomplished this feat, all the arguments for turning back by mid-January were never again discussed.

Magellan was overwhelmed. The captain general, Pigafetta recorded, "wept for joy." When he recovered, he named the just-discovered Pacific cape "Cape Desire, for we had been desiring it for a long time." The marvelous but hazardous strait itself lacked a name. At first, the men simply called it the strait. By 1527, six years after Magellan's death and the expedition's conclusion, the waterway had earned the name by which it is still known, the Strait of Magellan. For all his pride, Magellan never dared to name the strait after himself.

On November 28, 1520, as the armada approached the Pacific, the seas turned gray and rough. It was late in the day, and the dull skies were fading to darkness as the three ships put the western mouth of the strait to stern.

For Magellan and his crew, it had been a remarkable rite of passage. Although the armada enjoyed reasonably good fortune, Magellan's extraordinary skill as a strategist proved to be the critical factor in negotiating the entire length of the strait. Magellan even relied on the taste of seawater to guide the fleet. As the water became fresher, he knew he was traveling inland, and once it turned salty, he realized he was approaching the Pacific.

Not even the loss of his best pilot, Estêvão Gomes, and his biggest ship, *San Antonio*, had defeated him; the more the fleet shrank, the more nimble it became. Magellan's approach to navigating uncharted waters went far beyond technical ability in boat handling and direction finding; it revealed an ability to invent original tactics to guide a fleet of ships through hundreds of miles of unmapped archipelagos in rough weather. Magellan's skill in negotiating the entire length of the strait is acknowledged as the single greatest feat in the history of maritime exploration.

Magellan set a course to the north, following the western coast of Chile, whose rugged mountains matched the Pacific for wildness and danger. The strait they had just left seemed like an enchanted refuge in comparison to the ocean they now faced.

The men of the Armada de Molucca looked on the scene with dread. They knew the voyage was far from over. No matter how great the feat of navigating the strait from one ocean to another, it would have little value unless the armada reached the Spice Islands. No one aboard the fleet's three remaining ships suspected they were about to traverse the largest body of water in the world to get there.

The Strait of Magellan seen from space in a NASA image.

CHAPTER EIGHT

A Race Against Death

The scale of the Pacific Ocean was past imagining to Magellan. It encompasses one-third of the earth's surface, covers twice the area of the Atlantic Ocean, and extends over a greater area than all the dry land on the planet. Lost in this immensity are twenty-five thousand islands, and beneath its waters lurks the lowest point on earth, the Mariana Trench, buried in inky blackness thirty-six thousand feet below the shimmering surface. The Pacific had had the same appearance and character for tens of millions of years before Magellan and his men ventured across its surface, yet they knew nothing of these geological wonders. The men of the Armada de Molucca might as well have been sailing across the dark side of the moon.

Magellan anticipated a short cruise to the Spice Islands followed by a longer but untroubled voyage home through familiar waters. He believed that his men had learned from their ordeals. The mutinies had weeded out the faint of heart and the uncooperative. The crew, once numbering 260 men and boys in five ships, now consisted of fewer than 200 in three vessels: *Trinidad*, still the flagship of the fleet; *Concepción*, where Juan Rodríguez Serrano ruled; and *Victoria*, under Duarte Barbosa's command. Still, Magellan had no idea of the real challenge ahead: one not of shoals or climate, but of distance.

Throughout December 1520 and most of January 1521, the days at sea went by for the crew as if they were in a trance. Life at sea—so uncertain during the Port Saint Julian mutiny and the intricate maneuvering through the strait—became routine, almost dull. From the first light of dawn, the crew kept time with an hourglass; when it was turned over, the pages sang their familiar incantations. Each day at noon the pilot Francisco Albo determined the fleet's latitude by shooting the sun—measuring its angle to the horizon—generally with considerable accuracy. Every evening, the other two captains went on deck, drew close to *Trinidad*, and saluted Magellan: *¡Dios vos salve, capitán-general y señor maestro y buona compaña!* The fleet's pilots relied on celestial navigation, using the Southern Cross and other constellations as their guide. Magellan, ever watchful, constantly double-checked their course, in case they changed direction under the cover of night.

Magellan and his captains held morning and evening prayers each day. The nights brought relief from the heat, and the sailors remained on deck to escape their cramped, stinking, and suffocating sleeping quarters. At rest, they observed the diamond-hard stars etched on the canopy of the heavens. Pigafetta turned his ever-curious mind to making astronomical observations: "The Antarctic Pole is not so starry as the Arctic. Many small stars clustered together are seen, which have the appearance of two clouds of mist."

Without realizing it, Pigafetta had just recorded an observation of great consequence. The "clouds of mist" he described are in fact two irregular dwarf galaxies orbiting our own galaxy and containing billions of stars enveloped in a gaseous blanket; they are known today as the Magellanic Clouds. To the naked eye, they look like pieces of the Milky Way torn off and flung across the heavens.

On December 18, 1520, Magellan changed course. The new course took the armada west, away from South America into the Pacific. Soon the mainland, hardly more than a smudge on the horizon, disappeared from view for good, increasing the crew's sense of isolation and anxiety. If there was ever a time for a monster to appear on the horizon, for the water to boil, or for a magnetic island to pull the nails from the hulls of their ships, this was it.

Nothing quite so supernatural occurred. Instead, the ships

encountered a different kind of miracle: steady winds at their back. Among Magellan's most crucial navigational decisions was to sail north, rather than west, after exiting the strait. As the ships reached higher and higher latitudes, the Pacific, so threatening when they first encountered it in the south, gradually transformed into a swelling silken sheet. The mysterious change was brought about by the Coriolis force: the earth's easterly rotation causes the wind to veer in a westerly direction. These are the trade winds, named for the crucial role they would play in aiding transoceanic trade routes. The fleet was getting the benefit of some of the steadiest winds on the planet.

The winds Magellan encountered still lacked a name, and the crew did not realize how extraordinary this current of air was until they had experienced it for some weeks. Magellan's discovery of the Pacific trade winds ranks among his major findings, and was perhaps his most useful.

For days on end, the waves slapped rhythmically against the hulls, the sails sighed and swelled contentedly in their fittings, and the seamen spent their idle hours playing card games or sleeping. Pigafetta occupied himself by attempting to speak with their captive, a cooperative Patagonian native. In the process, he became the first European to learn and to transcribe the Tehuelche language of Patagonia. Hour after hour, the tall, bronzed, clean-shaven, nearly naked Patagonian huddled in earnest conversation with the much shorter and paler European in his breeches and loose-fitting shirt, scratching eagerly with his pen. Gesturing with hands and fingers, the two of them engaged in a game of mutual understanding, surrounded by an ocean of unbelievable dimensions.

Pigafetta's collaboration with the giant resulted in a phrase book called *Words of the Patagonian Giants*. "All these words are pronounced in the throat," the chronicler advised, "for they pronounce them thus." Pigafetta began with the Tehuelche word for "head," which he transcribed as *her*. "Eyes" sounded to him like *other*. "Nose": *or*. "Ears": *sane*. "Mouth": *xiam*. And so on through subjects of interest to him.

Pigafetta's phrase book lacked the commercial value of spices or gold, or the prestige of conquered territories, but it marked the beginning of the modern study of linguistics, and to later generations of scholars it would offer clues to the migrations of various tribes across the South American continent.

———————

Pigafetta also introduced his cooperative prisoner to Catholicism. "I made the sign of the cross," Pigafetta recalled. The man intuited that the cross represented a spiritual power, and eventually Pigafetta persuaded him that it symbolized a source of strength rather than danger.

Around that time, the Patagonian began to weaken and fell ill. No one could say what sickened him—Pigafetta did not record any symptoms; perhaps it was the change of diet or an illness he caught from the Europeans. The sicker he became, the more he relied on the cross. Pigafetta gave him a real cross to hold, and, as instructed, the man brought it to his lips, seeking its strength and healing power. But the illness worsened, and it became clear that he was dying. Pigafetta persuaded the prisoner to convert to Christianity. He was baptized, and the man, whose original name Pigafetta never mentioned, became known as Paul. He died shortly thereafter, a Patagonian Christian who met a unique and tragic fate.

———————

Although the weather remained perfect, the winds strong and constant, the armada failed to encounter islands with food and water. They had passed east of the Juan Fernández Islands, then north of the Marshall Islands of Bikar, Bikini, and Eniwetok. Had their course varied by only a few degrees south, they would have been able to explore Easter Island or, farther west, the Society Islands' Tahiti. At the same time, the fleet also narrowly avoided marine hazards such as razor-sharp reefs that could have sliced into their hulls.

Thirst and hunger tormented the crew. The seals they had butchered and salted in Patagonia turned rotten and became infested with maggots, which devoured sails, rigging, and even the sailors' clothes, rendering them all useless. Pigafetta chronicled, "We ate biscuit which was no longer biscuit, but powder of biscuits swarming with worms, for they had eaten the good. It stank strongly of the urine of rats. We drank yellow water that had been putrid for many days. Rats were sold for one-half ducado apiece, and even then we could not get them."

The rats commanded a premium because sailors believed that eating them might offer protection against the disease they all feared: scurvy. Scurvy posed the single greatest danger to the health of the men during the voyage. There was no known cure, and if unchecked, it could claim the lives of them all.

One by one, the men began to suffer from the disease. A sense of exhaustion gradually overtook them, and their gums began to feel sore and spongy. When they pushed with their tongues, even gently, their teeth wobbled. As the disease progressed, their teeth began to fall out, and their gums bled uncontrollably and festered with painful boils. No one knew then what caused these symptoms and the suffering that followed.

Even though they suffered terribly, sailors were still expected to work. If they failed to appear for their shift, the boatswain whipped them with the end of a rope and then dragged them up on deck, where the sunlight pitilessly revealed their deteriorated condition. Their skin seemed to be separating from their bones, and old scars and sores, long healed, reopened. Their bodies were literally falling apart.

As scurvy claimed one life after another, burials at sea became commonplace. Sailors, many of them suffering from the early stages of scurvy themselves, wrapped the body in the remnant of an old, tattered sail, secured it with rope, and tied cannonballs to the feet. A priest and, on occasion, the captain uttered a brief prayer; two sailors lifted the corpse onto a plank, tilted it, and committed their crewmate's mortal remains to the deep.

The intense suffering could have been prevented by daily dose of one spoonful of lemon juice; that is the amount of vitamin C necessary to prevent scurvy. Humans need regular infusions of vitamin C to synthesize protein-based connective tissues such as skin, ligaments, tendons, and bones, which give our bodies tensile strength.

While their men suffered and died around them (twenty-nine, in addition to the sole remaining Indian passenger they had captured), Magellan, Pigafetta, and several other officers remained mysteriously healthy. The officers regularly dipped into their supply of quince jam without realizing it contained vitamin C and was actually a potent antiscorbutic. Since Magellan was known for personally taking care of his men when they became ill, he would likely have insisted on giving them daily rations of quince, had he known of its benefits.

The armada's first landfall occurred on January 24, 1521. It turned out to be disappointing: a simple island rising mysteriously from the ocean. Magellan named it San Pablo because the sighting occurred on the Feast of the Conversion of Saint Paul. The island proved useless to Magellan's vessels; he saw neither evidence of human habitation nor a safe place to drop anchor. After sailing completely around the island, he signaled the ships to proceed on their course. San Pablo could not come to their aid.

Even Magellan, normally possessed of superhuman determination and indifference to hardship, became depressed and unstable as the transpacific crossing wore on. In a rage, he flung his useless maps overboard, crying, "With the pardon of the cartographers, the Moluccas are not to be found in their appointed place!"

Unable to make a landfall, the ships were carried by substantial trade winds over astounding distances. On February 13 they crossed the equator. Magellan was utterly confused by this time. He had expected to reach the Spice Islands long before this point in the voyage; according to the maps he had studied, he had already covered the entire Pacific Ocean and should have been in Asia by now.

Worse, he had entered Portuguese waters, as defined by the

Treaty of Tordesillas; if he discovered that the Spice Islands lay squarely within Portuguese territory, the finding would defeat the purpose of the expedition and he could not claim them for Spain. To add to the pressure, he was running out of water, and his men were still dying of scurvy.

————

Deliverance finally came ninety-eight days after the fleet left the strait. At about 6:00 a.m. on March 21, 1521, two landmasses slowly rose from the sea; they appeared to be about twenty-five miles away. Eventually, a third mass came into view. From his perch in a crow's nest sixty feet above deck, Lope Navarro, *Victoria's* lookout, peered into the hazy glow, trying to distinguish between these promising outlines and mere cloud formations. Throughout that anxious morning, the ships sailed directly for the shapes at a rate of six knots.

When Navarro was convinced of the masses' true nature, he announced from on high, "*¡Tierra!*" Land!

"*¡Tierra, tierra!*" The shrill cry tore through the silent morning. "*¡Tierra!*"

CHAPTER NINE

– A VANISHED EMPIRE –

P hysically and emotionally exhausted, Magellan climbed partway to the crow's nest to see the prospect for himself. His men raised their shaggy heads to glimpse their salvation. As the islands became clearer in the morning light, the lookout shouted again, "¡Tierra!" and gestured to the south, where cliffs rose from the sea. Overjoyed, Magellan awarded the fortunate lookout a bonus of one hundred ducats.

The first landmass Navarro had spotted was likely the mountainous Rota, one of the islands in the volcanic archipelago now called the Mariana Islands, which lie about three thousand miles west of the Hawaiian Islands. Thanks to the earth's curvature and the angle from which the armada approached, Rota initially appeared to be two islands. The other island, the one where the armada would eventually land, was Guam, the largest of the Marianas.

For Magellan, the landfall on Guam came as a mixed blessing. Although the island provided relief from the misery he and his men had endured during their ninety-eight day Pacific cruise, nothing about it suggested they were anywhere near their goal, the Spice Islands. Nevertheless, it was land. Since leaving the western mouth of the strait, Magellan had traveled more than seven thousand miles without interruption—the longest ocean voyage recorded until that time.

———

On Wednesday, March 6, the armada approached "a small island in the north-west direction, and two others lying to the south-west," Pigafetta wrote. The crew was amazed by the "many small sailboats approaching us, and they were going so fast they seemed to fly."

The sailors were getting their first look at the outrigger canoe known as a proa, and often called a flying proa because it was able to attain speeds of up to twenty knots and seemed to fly over the water's

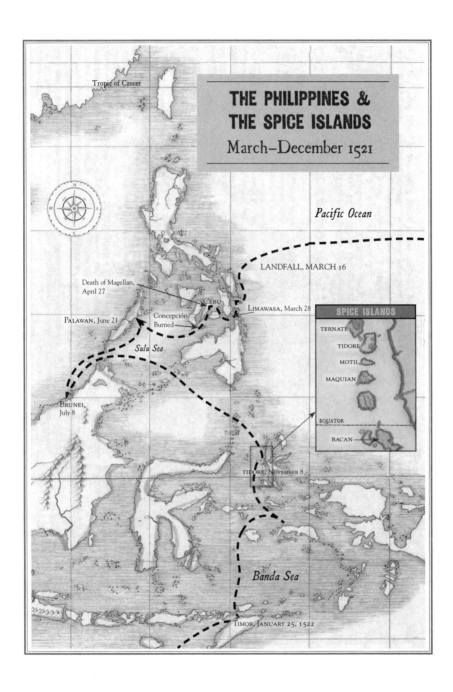

THE PHILIPPINES &
THE SPICE ISLANDS
March–December 1521

Tropic of Cancer

Pacific Ocean

LANDFALL, MARCH 16

Death of Magellan,
April 27

CEBU

LIMAWASA, March 28

SPICE ISLANDS

PALAWAN, June 21

Concepción
Burned

TERNATE

TIDORE

Sulu Sea

MOTIL

MAQUIAN

BRUNEI,
July 8

EQUATOR

BACAN

TIDORE, NOVEMBER 8

Banda Sea

TIMOR, JANUARY 25, 1522

An illustration from Pigafetta's journal depicts Guam and the quick, highly maneuverable vessels called proas that were sailed by inhabitants of the Pacific islands.

surface. The proas approaching Magellan's fleet were manned by a Polynesian tribe now known as the Chamorro people, although this was not the name by which they were known in Magellan's day. At first, Magellan's crew referred to all the tribes they encountered in the Pacific as *Indios* (Indians), in the mistaken belief that the Indies must be nearby.

Four hours after sighting land, the Armada de Molucca, surrounded by a welcoming party of flying proas, entered a deep turquoise lagoon of unusually warm, clear water. As they approached, the sailors could see beaches, rocky cliffs, and steep, thickly forested slopes. The moment of contact between two societies, until now completely clueless of each other's existence, had finally arrived.

———

At first, the Chamorros—hundreds of them—surrounded the fleet. Taller and stronger than the Europeans, they boarded the flagship and stole everything they could—rigging, crockery, weapons, and anything made of iron. The crew, in their weakened condition, pleaded with Magellan to force the islanders to leave. Eventually, a fight broke out, with the Chamorros wielding sticks and the Europeans shooting arrows.

While this was happening, a second wave of Chamorros skimmed across the water in their proas, and, to the Europeans' astonishment, distributed food to the starving sailors. Once they had fed the Europeans, the Chamorros took up their sticks and fighting began again, this time more viciously. Magellan, "seeing that the number of people was increasing, ordered those in the ship to stop throwing arrows; with this, the Indians stopped." His show of restraint turned out to be just the right gesture.

If only matters had ended on this peaceful note. Unaccustomed to European concepts of trade and property, the Chamorros, while happy to feed the sailors, did not understand that, to the Europeans, some things aboard ship were simply off-limits. The Chamorros stole Magellan's own dinghy. The next day, taking the robbery as a personal insult, Magellan ordered forty men into the two remaining longboats. The crews reached the shore—the first landing by Europeans on an inhabited Pacific island. Then they went on a rampage, burning homes and killing men.

The stunned Chamorros offered no resistance. "When we wounded many of this kind of people with our arrows," Pigafetta wrote, "they looked at the arrow, and then drew it forth with much astonishment, and immediately afterwards they died." In the midst of the bloodshed, Magellan recovered his dinghy.

———

The European visitors were surprised to find that the Chamorros possessed very few weapons. They did carry a stick with a fishbone attached to one end, but it was for catching flying fish, not for combat. It now appeared that the armada's initial encounter with the Chamorros might have been a tragic misunderstanding. The Chamorros—fascinated by *Trinidad's* skiff because it resembled their own canoes—had no concept of private property, so they believed the newcomers' possessions belonged to one and all. On this basis, they had been equally pleased to share their food and supplies with the starving intruders. Nevertheless, the captain general christened the island, as well as two others nearby, the Islas de los Ladrones (Islands of the Thieves). A more accurate name might have been the Islands of the Sharers.

———

On March 9, 1521, as the armada left the island, the Chamorros reacted with anger, perhaps feeling insulted or betrayed by the unexpected departure. Over a hundred proas took to the water. "They approached our ships, showing us fish, and feigning to give it to us," Pigafetta wrote. "But they threw stones at us, and then ran away."

Once again, the fleet plunged blindly into the vast western Pacific. Magellan set a westward course, journeying deeper into the unexplored reaches of the ocean in his quest for the Moluccas. The fleet enjoyed another marvelous week of sailing downwind.

On March 16, a lookout spied the mountains of a large island rising from the sea. The fleet had reached the eastern edge of the Philippine archipelago—over three thousand islands, most of which cover less than a square mile. The Philippines are situated almost directly south of Japan and north of Borneo. Magellan sensed he was getting close to the Spice Islands, but he did not realize how close.

———

Most Western accounts of Philippine history begin abruptly in 1521, with Magellan's arrival. But centuries before, these islands were well-known to Chinese and Arab traders, who, with their superior sailing technology, traveled among them and developed sophisticated trading networks with the native societies. Archeological evidence suggests that trade between mainland Asia and the Philippines had become highly developed as early as 1000 CE. Chinese sailboats, distinguished by their three tall feather-like sails stiffened with wood, became a familiar and welcome sight in the Philippines. The constant commerce in the Philippine archipelago brought islanders out of their isolation and spread Asian cultural influences, especially writing, along with their goods. By the time Magellan arrived, Filipinos who dwelled near the ocean and inland waterways had long been literate.

Chinese exploration of the Philippines reached its commercial peak during the years 1405 to 1433, when the Treasure Fleet ruled the South Pacific and the Indian Ocean. The fleet's enormous ships traveled as far as the east coast of Africa to collect precious items and tributes for the emperor. They were eight or nine times longer than Columbus's ships and five or six times longer than any in Magellan's armada. The fleet was the creation of one man whose accomplishments rivaled and in some ways surpassed the exploits of Columbus and Magellan: Zheng He.

Zheng He was a giant of a man, seven feet tall, with a strong personality to match his physique. His complexion was said to be "rough like the surface of an orange," and "his eyebrows were like swords and his forehead wide, like a tiger's." He oversaw a fleet consisting of fifteen hundred wooden ships, including the largest sail-powered vessels ever built. They were extraordinarily luxurious, with staterooms, gold fittings, bronze cannons (for display rather than combat), and silk furnishings. Their seaworthiness was greatly enhanced by bulkheads, watertight compartments whose design was inspired by the chambers of the bamboo stalk. It would be several centuries before Western ships used the same technology.

Unlike the Armada de Molucca, the Treasure Fleet did not conquer or claim distant lands. Although the Chinese considered themselves culturally superior to the outside world, they had no interest in establishing a colonial or military empire. Rather, the goal was to establish trade and diplomatic relations with the "barbarians" beyond their borders and to conduct scientific research. They built trading posts and warehouses wherever they went. The Treasure Fleet established and maintained the first international maritime trading network and explored the African coast all the way from Mozambique to the Persian Gulf, and across many other points throughout Southeast Asia and India.

Zheng He's voyages demonstrated that China was the most powerful nation in the world, a seagoing empire that Spain or Portugal would have feared and envied had they known of its reach and power. But upon Zheng He's death, around 1433, the Chinese abandoned the Treasure Fleet and destroyed its vessels, and its reputation never reached European shores. Portuguese and Spanish explorers sailed into the vacuum left by China. Like the Chinese, they came in search of wealth—but quite unlike them, they fiercely battled for territory, for commercial and political advantage over one another, and for religious conquest.

Magellan, like other Europeans, had no direct knowledge of the Treasure Fleet, but he and his men kept stumbling across artifacts of the vanished Chinese empire: silk, porcelain, writing, and sophisticated weights and measures were everywhere in evidence. The era of Chinese colonization had ended; the era of Spanish colonization was just beginning.

———

The sprawling Philippine archipelago did not appear on European maps, and neither Magellan nor his pilots knew what to make of their discovery. It was the fifth Sunday of Lent, with Easter fast approaching. Lent was dedicated to Lazarus, who had risen from the dead, and like him, the surviving crew members had overcome illness to regain their strength and persevere. Magellan decided to name the archipelago after Lazarus, but his inspiration did not last. Twenty-one years later, another European explorer, Ruy López de Villalobos, renamed it Las Islas Filipinas (the Philippines), after King Philip II of Spain.

On Monday, March 18, Magellan's crew saw a boat carrying nine men approach. Calculating the potential risks and rewards of their second encounter with the peoples of the Pacific, Magellan made sure his men's weapons were ready. Meanwhile, he assembled a different sort of arsenal: shiny trinkets, in case the encounter turned out to be peaceful.

This time, Magellan handled the situation confidently. "The captain, seeing that these people were reasonable, ordered that they be given food and drink, and he presented them with red caps, mirrors, combs, bells, . . . and other things," Pigafetta wrote. "And when those people saw the captain's fair dealing, they gave him fish and a jar of palm wine, figs more than a foot long [bananas] and other smaller ones of better flavor, and two coconuts. . . . And they made signs with their hands that in four days they would bring us rice, coconuts, and sundry other food."

Perhaps they had found paradise, or at least a break from an expedition now in its third year. Magellan fed coconut milk supplied by the generous Filipinos to the sailors still suffering from scurvy. Their idyll lasted a week, each day bringing with it new discoveries and a growing intimacy with their friendly Filipino hosts. But Magellan nearly destroyed the tranquillity when he invited the Filipinos aboard *Trinidad*. He showed them "all his merchandise, namely cloves, cinnamon, pepper, walnut, nutmeg, ginger, mace, gold, and all that was in the ship." Clearly he felt he was no longer among thieves, and his trust was thoroughly rewarded when the Filipinos appeared to recognize these

An illustration from The Boxer Codex, *first printed in about 1590, that vividly depicts a scene encountered by the Armada de Molucca: a European ship in the Philippines is approached by native craft, their occupants offering fish, fruits, and other goods for trade.*

exotic and precious spices and tried to explain where they grew locally, the first indication that the armada was approaching the Spice Islands. Magellan's reaction can be easily imagined. Perhaps he would reach the Moluccas after all.

He then honored his guests, or so he thought, by ordering his gunners to discharge their artillery. The roar shattered the silence and echoed against the distant hills, terrifying the Filipinos. Was Magellan trying to impress these defenseless islanders, and himself, with the power of his weapons? Magellan quickly reassured the frightened Filipinos and coaxed them into remaining on board; at the same time,

he enjoyed the absolute power his weapons gave him, should he ever feel the need to use them.

————

On Monday, March 25, Magellan gave the order to weigh anchor and the three black ships headed out of the harbor on a west-southwest course, deeper into the Philippine archipelago.

The following night, the crew spied an island distinguished by a dull red glow, the unmistakable sign of campfires, and they knew they were not alone. In the morning, Magellan decided to risk approaching, and in a now familiar ritual, they were greeted by another small boat, this one carrying eight warriors with unknown intentions.

Magellan's slave, Enrique, addressed them in a Malay language, and to Magellan's astonishment, the men appeared to understand him, and replied in the same tongue. Magellan had acquired Enrique ten years earlier in Malacca. If Enrique had originally come from these islands, been captured as a boy by slave raiders from Sumatra, and sold to Magellan at a slave mart in Malacca, the chain of circumstances would explain his understanding the local language. But beyond that, it meant that Magellan's servant was, in fact, the first person to circle the world and return home.

The captain general attempted to entice the islanders with a "red cap and other things tied to a bit of wood." Still, they remained at a distance, refusing the gifts. Finally, Magellan's peace offerings were set out on a plank and pushed in the canoe's direction. The men in the boat enthusiastically seized the gifts and paddled back to shore, where, Magellan assumed, they showed their trophies to their ruler.

"About two hours later we saw two *balanghai* coming," Pigafetta wrote. "They are large boats . . . full of men, and their king was in the larger of them, being seated under an awning of mats. When the king came near the flagship, the slave spoke to him. The king understood him. He ordered some of his men to enter the ships, but he always remained in his *balanghai*, at some little distance from the ship, until his own men returned; and as soon as they returned he departed."

Magellan tried to conduct himself as a gracious visitor, but he was outdone by the generosity of the king, who offered a "large bar of gold and a basketful of ginger." Magellan politely yet firmly refused to accept this tribute, but he moved his ships closer to the king's hut for the night, as a symbol of their newfound allegiance.

This encounter with indigenous people was shaping up as the armada's most peaceful and successful since their joyful layover in Rio de Janeiro. A king willing to give gold and ginger might have other resources, but experience had shown that first impressions could be misleading, if not outright dangerous.

———————

The next day, Good Friday of 1521, Magellan put his relationship with the islanders to the test. He sent Enrique ashore on the island of Limasawa. Even today, as part of the province of Southern Leyte in the Philippines, Limasawa is a remote, inaccessible island consisting of six square miles of sand with broad, clean, inviting beaches; unusual rock formations; and caves. Although Magellan was the first European explorer to reach Limasawa, he was not the first outsider to find safe harbor here.

Without realizing it, he had arrived at an important trading post. Chinese traders had been visiting the island for five centuries, their junks (sailing ships of Chinese design) carrying sophisticated manufactured items such as porcelain, silk, and lead sinkers; the islanders traded for these items with products from their beaches and forests: cotton, wax, pearls, betel nuts, tortoise shells, coconuts, sweet potatoes, and coconut-leaf mats. The Limasawans enjoyed a reputation for hospitality and, more important, honesty. So the appearance of the armada, while unusual, was not wholly unexpected by the islanders, who were prepared to trade with their guests.

Once he was ashore, Enrique asked the Limasawan ruler, Rajah Kolambu, to send more food to the fleet, for which payment would be given. The king responded favorably to the request and came himself, along with "six or eight men," all of whom boarded the flagship. "He embraced the captain general to whom he gave three porcelain jars covered with leaves and full of raw rice, two very large *orades*"—the dorado, a fish. In return, Magellan "gave the king a garment of red and yellow cloth made in the Turkish fashion, and a fine red cap. . . . Then the captain general had a collation spread for them, and told the king through a slave that he desired to be *casicasi* with him. The king replied that he also wished to enter the same relations with the captain general."

This was a strong statement. To be *casicasi* meant that Magellan wished to become blood brothers with the island king. "Both cut their chests, and the blood was poured in a vessel and mixed together with wine, and each of them drank one half of it."

Magellan's attitude toward indigenous people had undergone a revolution. Where he had been willing to convert, kidnap, and, when it suited him, even kill the giants of Patagonia, he felt a genuine unusual kinship with this Filipino ruler. He took the king into his confidence and was soon trying to explain how the Armada de Molucca had navigated its way across the globe.

———

To impress the Limasawan king, Magellan gave an astonishing demonstration. He brought out one of his men, dressed in armor from his knees to his neck. Then three other Europeans, "armed with swords and daggers . . . struck him on all parts of the body." As the blows fell off the armor, "the king was rendered speechless." The king seemed to think the Europeans possessed superhuman powers. No man could have withstood the shower of blows, yet the armored soldier had done just that.

Satisfied by the king's reaction, Magellan instructed Enrique, his slave and translator, to tell the king that "one of those armed men was worth one hundred of his own men" and boasted that his armada brought with it two hundred warriors equipped with armor and weapons. The message was plain: a wise leader should keep Magellan as an ally rather than antagonize him. Recovering from the shock of what he had seen, the king quickly agreed that a single warrior in armor was worth one hundred natives.

To complement their huge collection of weapons, literally thousands, enough for a small army, the fleet carried a hundred sets of armor (rather than the two hundred Magellan had claimed). Magellan had brought along his own set of deluxe armor, which included a coat of mail, body armor, and six swords for his personal use. His helmet was topped with bright plumage. With their firearms and armor, Magellan believed they were the masters of all they surveyed, a belief that would cost him dearly.

———

Once Magellan finished his military display, he formally requested that two representatives inspect the island's huts and food stores. The king complied, and the captain general chose Pigafetta and another crew member.

The moment he stepped ashore, Pigafetta encountered luxury the likes of which he had not seen since leaving Spain. "When I reached the shore, the king . . . made a regal spectacle," he reported. Kolambu's hair, "exceedingly black," hung to his shoulders, and he wore two large golden earrings. "He wore a cotton cloth all embroidered with silk, which covered him from the waist to the knees. He had three spots of gold on every tooth, and his teeth appeared as if bound with gold." Tattoos covered every inch of his glistening, perfumed body.

The women, Pigafetta noticed, "are clad in tree cloth from their waist down, and their hair is black and reaches to the ground. They have holes pierced in their ears which are filled with gold." Gold was everywhere—in jewelry, goblets, and dishes—and was readily mined on the island in "pieces as large as walnuts and eggs."

Everyone, it seemed, chewed constantly on a fruit that resembled a pear. This "fruit" was the betel nut, actually the seed of a type of palm tree. "It makes the mouth exceedingly red. All the people in those parts of the world use it, for it is very cooling to the heart, and if they ceased to use it they would die."

Pigafetta had little time to gawk. "The king took me by the hand . . . and they led us under a bamboo covering, where there was a balanghai as long as eighty of my palm lengths. The king's men stood about us in a circle with swords, daggers, spears, and bucklers. The king had a plate of pork brought in and a large jar filled with wine. At every mouthful, we drank a cup of wine."

Dinner was announced; it was a royal feast. Out of respect for the king, Pigafetta, an observant Catholic, forced himself to overlook one of his own religious customs. "I ate meat on Holy Friday," he confessed, "for I could not help myself."

After the meal, "we went to the palace of the king"—in reality, a "hay loft thatched with banana and palm leaves. It was built up high from the ground on huge posts of wood and it was necessary to ascend it by means of ladders." Once everyone had clambered inside the flimsy structure, "the king made us sit down there on a bamboo mat with our feet drawn up like tailors. The king's eldest son, who was the prince, came over to us, whereupon the king told him to sit down near us, and he accordingly did so." More feasting followed. Eventually, the king went to bed, leaving the prince behind. Pigafetta slept in the rickety palace on bamboo mats "with pillows made of leaves."

In the morning, the king returned, took Pigafetta "by the hand" once more and offered him another lavish meal, but before the feasting could resume, the longboat came to get the Europeans. One of the king's brothers, the king of another island, and three other men accompanied Pigafetta and the other crew member back to the armada.

———

On the morning of Easter Sunday, the Europeans explained the importance of the occasion to the king. Impressed, he and his royal brother sent two freshly slaughtered pigs. And then some of the islanders decided to worship alongside them.

According to Pigafetta, "The mass was celebrated. The kings went forward to kiss the cross as we did, but they did not participate in the Eucharist. The ships fired all their artillery at once when the body of Christ was elevated, the signal having been given from the shore with muskets. After the conclusion of the mass, some of our men took communion."

After the solemn ceremony, it was time to celebrate. To amuse and impress his hosts, Magellan organized a fencing tournament, "at which the kings were greatly pleased." Next, Magellan ordered his men to display the cross, complete with "nails and the crown" and explained to the kings that his own sovereign, King Charles, had given these objects to him, "so that wherever he might go he might set up those tokens." Now he wished to set up the cross on their island. Magellan wanted to place the cross "on the summit of the highest mountain," and he explained the many benefits of displaying it as he proposed. For one thing, "neither thunder, nor lightning, nor storms would harm them in the least," and for another, "if any of their men were captured, they would be set free immediately on that sign being shown." The kings accepted the cross as a totem, apparently without having any idea of what it actually meant.

The discussion turned to politics. Magellan asked if the king had any enemies; if so, Magellan would "go with his ships to destroy them and render them obedient." As it happened, the king said there were "two islands hostile to him, but . . . it was not the season to go there." Hearing this, Magellan turned warlike: "The captain general told him that if God would again allow him to return to those districts, he would bring so many men that he would make the king's enemies subject to him by force."

Nothing in Magellan's charter from King Charles mentioned fighting tribal wars or mass conversions to Christianity; he was supposed to "go in search of the Strait," demonstrate that the Spice Islands belonged to Spain, and return in ships filled with spices. Now he put aside his commercial goals in favor of conversions and conquest. Determined to form an alliance with friendly local rulers by making war on their enemies, he hoped to strengthen their bond and establish a permanent Spanish presence in the newly discovered archipelago.

Considering his work done, Magellan announced his intention to depart in the morning. Despite all the pigs and rice and wine the kings had given him, the captain general declared he needed even more food, and the kings recommended the island of Cebu as a convenient place to forage.

CHAPTER TEN

— THE FINAL BATTLE —

A s the Armada de Molucca approached the shores of Cebu, the
crew watched village after village emerge from the obscurity of
the jungle as if by magic. The inhabitants looked peaceful and not
particularly startled by the appearance of strange ships. Their elaborate
huts, rising on stilts in groups of five or six, resembled homesteads or
even small estates.

The armada searched for a convenient anchorage. When they had
been secured, the three black ships suddenly erupted with thunder and
smoke, terrifying the local people observing from the shore.

Magellan sent his son, Cristóvão Rebêlo, as an ambassador to the
king of Cebu, along with the slave Enrique to serve as an interpreter.
Enrique explained that it was their custom to discharge their
weapons "when entering such places, as a sign of peace and friendship."
His words had their intended effect, and soon the king, Humabon, was
asking what he could do for them. Enrique said that his captain owed
allegiance to the "greatest king and prince in the world, and that he
was going to discover the Moluccas." He added that his captain had
decided to pass this way "because of the good report which he had of
him from the king of Limasawa and to buy food." Impressed, Humabon
welcomed the visitors, but, he advised, "It was their custom for all ships
that entered their ports to pay tribute." Only four days before, a ship
from Siam "laden with gold and slaves" had called on the island and
paid its tribute.

Magellan—through Enrique—insisted that *his* king, the king of
Spain, was the greatest in all the world, and the Armada de Molucca
would never pay tribute to a lesser ruler. He declared, "If the king
wished peace he would have peace, but if war instead, [then he would
have] war."

The king shrewdly agreed to discuss matters with his chieftains, and the next morning he offered to pay tribute to the "most powerful king in the world," rather than demanding it for himself. The standoff had ended. Magellan announced to Humabon that he would "trade with him and no others." Prompted by the king of Limasawa, Humabon offered to become blood brothers with Magellan; the captain general had only to send "a drop of his blood from his right arm, and he would do the same as a sign of the most sincere friendship."

———

Relations between the two proceeded well. The king's nephew came aboard *Trinidad*, accompanied by an entourage of eight chieftains, to swear loyalty. Holding court, Magellan played the part of a noble ruler with gusto: "The captain general was seated in a red velvet chair, the principal men of the ships on leather chairs, and the others on mats upon the floor. . . . The captain general said many things concerning peace, and that he prayed to God to confirm it in heaven. They said they had never heard such words, but that they took great pleasure in hearing them. The captain general, seeing that they listened and answered willingly, began to advance arguments to induce them to accept the faith."

His speech must have been persuasive because "all joyfully entreated the captain general to leave them two men, or at least one, to instruct them in the faith." Magellan explained that he could not leave anyone behind with them, but, if they wished, the armada's chaplain, Father Valderrama, would gladly baptize the Cebuans, and when they returned, they would bring priests and friars to instruct them. He cautioned the Cebuans not to convert to Christianity simply to win his favor, and promised not to "cause any displeasure to those who wished to live according to their own law." But, he said, the Christians would get special treatment. "All cried out with one voice that they were not becoming Christians through fear or to please us," Pigafetta recorded, "but of their own free will." Magellan was so encouraged by this response that he promised to leave behind a suit of armor—just one— in gratitude.

After mutual assurances and reassurances had been exchanged, it was time for another feast. The Cebuan women performed an elaborate blessing before slaughtering the hogs. In return for their hospitality, Magellan presented to the king's nephew a bolt of white linen, a red cap, strings of glass beads, and a gilded glass cup. By the time the feast ended, the Cebuans regarded Magellan as something more than a man; he was a powerful god. The adulation rubbed off on the captain general, who increasingly believed himself to be divinely inspired, his expedition a demonstration of God's will. It was a dangerous delusion.

———

On Sunday morning, April 14, King Humabon was baptized. His baptismal ceremony unfolded with all the pageantry Magellan could muster. In the village square the day before, crew members had constructed a platform decorated with palm branches and other vegetation. A group of forty seamen, including Pigafetta, clambered into the longboats. Two wore gleaming armor and stood just behind the king of Spain's banner as it waved in the gentle ocean breeze. Having given fair warning, the crew discharged their weapons at the moment they went ashore, marking the formal commencement of the solemn occasion.

After the priest baptized him, Humabon took the name of Charles, after Magellan's sovereign. The baptism was more successful than Magellan had dared to hope. However, the king confessed that his chieftains still resisted the idea of becoming Christian.

The captain general instantly sent for the unruly chieftains and, as Pigafetta tells it, warned that "unless they obeyed the king as their king, he would have them killed, and would give their possessions to the king." This admonition completely contradicted Magellan's earlier promise that no one would be forced to become a Christian. Furthermore, baptism of adults was supposed to be voluntary and based on faith, not fear. In any event, the chieftains swiftly agreed to obey Magellan and convert.

Satisfied, Magellan announced that when he returned from Spain, he would bring so many soldiers with him that the king would be

112

recognized "as the greatest king of those regions, as he had been the first to express a determination to become a Christian." Swept along by Magellan's passion, the king lifted his hands to the sky, profusely thanked the captain general, and even asked again that some of his sailors stay behind to instruct the others in Christianity. This time Magellan agreed and said he would choose two men to stay here with the king, but in return he wished to take "two children of the chiefs with him" to visit Spain, learn Spanish, and describe the wonders of that country on their return to Cebu.

———

After dinner, the women took their turn at conversion. Father Valderrama, along with Pigafetta and several crew members, returned to the island to baptize the queen, who brought an entourage of forty women. She made a regal impression on the Europeans. "She was young and beautiful," Pigafetta noted, "and was entirely covered with a white and black cloth. Her mouth and nails were very red, while on her head she wore a large hat of palm leaves in the manner of a parasol, with a crown about it of the same leaves, like the tiara of the pope." She was given the name Johanna, after the Spanish king's mother.

In the following days, the entire population of Cebu embraced Christianity. In all, 2,200 souls converted of their own free will, without a shot being fired in anger. The scenes of conversion seemed touching and inspiring at first glance, but what significance the baptismal rite held for the Cebuans can only be imagined. Theater had won the day. Thousands of islanders had converted to Christianity, but for how long?

———

By mid-April 1521, Magellan was at his peak. He had overcome vicious mutinies, made good on his promise to discover the strait, navigated uncharted reaches of the Pacific Ocean, and claimed the Philippines, among other lands, for Spain, converting thousands of islanders in the process. But his unpredictable behavior—sometimes generous, sometimes reckless, occasionally both—suggests that his accomplishments had gone to his head. Throughout the voyage, he had displayed a fondness for religion, but he now went further, threatening to kill those who defied his crusade. Learning that there were chieftains on the neighboring island of Mactan who refused to convert, Magellan sent word that if they did not convert immediately and swear allegiance to King Charles, he would confiscate their property, a European concept that was nearly meaningless to the islanders, and punish them with death, a threat they understood but chose to ignore.

Magellan sent a group of his men to Mactan, where they set a village on fire. As the huts burned and the inhabitants fled, Magellan forced the rulers to swear obedience to Humabon, who in turn had to swear loyalty to the king of Spain.

Still, Magellan was worried the conversions might be undone. Despite his orders, for example, the locals had failed to burn their idols; in fact, they continued to make sacrifices to them, and he demanded to know why. Everywhere Magellan looked, there seemed to be an idol mocking him.

In their defense, the islanders explained that they were asking the gods to aid a sick man; he was so sick that he had been unable to speak for four days. He was not just any man—he was the prince's brother, considered the "bravest and wisest" on the entire island. But Christianity could not help him, because he had not been baptized.

Magellan seized on the illness to demonstrate the healing power of Christian faith. Burn your idols, he commanded, believe in Christ, and only Christ. If the sick man is baptized, he went on, "he would quickly recover." Magellan further claimed that if the sick man failed to recover, he would allow Humabon to "behead him, then and there." In fact, he would insist. Humabon, compliant as always, "replied that he would do it, for he truly believed in Christ."

Magellan prepared carefully. Once again, Pigafetta was in the thick of things and later wrote his impressions: "We baptized him and his two wives, and ten girls. Then the captain general asked him how he felt. He spoke immediately and said that by the grace of our Lord he felt very well. That was a most manifest miracle." The miraculous healing made a tremendous impression on the islanders, who now respected Magellan as they would a god. He was more powerful than their idols, yet he walked among them.

Before five days the sick man began to walk. In the following days, Magellan destroyed other idols displayed along the shore and forced the islanders to follow his example. The campaign to rid the island of idols consumed Magellan and the Cebuans, who vowed to burn all they could find, even the idols lurking in Humabon's house.

———

On April 26, Mactan's chief, Sula, sent one of his sons to Cebu, where he presented Magellan with an offering of two goats. He would have brought more, he explained, but the king with whom he shared the island, Lapu Lapu, had refused him. Lapu Lapu was the unruly chieftain who had resisted converting to Christianity and whose village Magellan had burned to the ground. He remained adamantly opposed to the European invader. Sula offered to place his soldiers at Magellan's disposal to fight Lapu Lapu: the combined forces might be able to get rid of him altogether. Magellan refused the offer and said he wanted to "see how the Spanish lions fought." He declared that he would send not one but three longboats filled with warriors.

Thanks to Magellan's arrogance, Sula came out the clear winner. Rather than Sula placing his soldiers at Magellan's disposal, Magellan now placed his men at Sula's service. The decision to fight threw the armada into a state of alarm. Magellan's inner circle immediately recognized that they had reached another turning point in the expedition. For the first time since their arrival in these lush islands, they seriously questioned Magellan's judgment, if not his sanity.

Converting natives was all to the good, but their primary mission was to reach the Spice Islands; that was what their orders from King Charles commanded them to do. Assembling a force large enough to face the islanders meant the ships would stand nearly empty and become vulnerable to attack; in the worst-case scenario, they might lose the battle and their ships. But no matter how many times they all asked Magellan to follow a peaceful and practical strategy, he refused to back down.

Magellan did make two minor changes. He reduced the number of men who were to serve Sula to a bare minimum, and he ordered his ships to keep far from shore. These crucial strategic decisions would place the entire enterprise at a tremendous disadvantage as the battle unfolded.

The captain general gave the order to prepare for attack, and his men wore armor, this time for actual combat, not for show. Their ranks included Pigafetta and Enrique. The Cebuans were under orders not to fight, but merely to observe the "Spanish lions" in their hunt for prey.

"At midnight," Pigafetta wrote, "sixty men of us set out armed with corselets and helmets, together with the Christian king, the prince, some of the chief men, and twenty or thirty *balanghais*. We reached Mactan three hours before dawn." Magellan decided that he did not wish to fight right away, which must have come as a relief to his apprehensive men, and he sent a message to Lapu Lapu saying that if the chieftain would simply "obey the king of Spain, recognize the Christian king as their sovereign, and pay us our tribute, he would be their friend; but that if they wished otherwise, they should wait to see how our lances wounded." This was the same arrangement Magellan had offered the other islanders, who had quickly accepted.

Lapu Lapu refused to yield and sent back a message boasting of his weapons' strength. At the same time, Lapu Lapu asked Magellan to postpone his attack "until morning, so that they might have more men." At first, Lapu Lapu's absurd request confused Magellan's men, but later it became clear it was a delaying tactic. As he considered the request and the possible motives behind it, Magellan lost precious time, along with the advantages of darkness.

Shallow water meant that the longboats had to keep away from the beach, which was bad enough; the increased distance from the longboats to the shore meant that Magellan's men would be exposed to Lapu Lapu's spears for a much longer period of time as they crossed to land. Worse, the big ships had to stay even farther back, in deep water, so far from the scene of battle that their crossbows and artillery would be useless.

———

By the time Magellan ordered his men to charge, dawn was breaking. As Magellan's men waded through the water to the beach, the Mactanese emerged from the jungle, numbering not in the dozens, as expected, but, according to Pigafetta's reckoning, fifteen hundred in all. The ratio of Mactanese fighters to Europeans was thirty to one. Magellan had boasted that just one of his armored men was worth a hundred island warriors; his estimate was about to be put to the test.

The ships' artillery, fired from a distance, did not reach the enemy. "The captain general cried . . . , 'Cease firing! Cease firing!'" but his command was ignored. The Europeans, weighed down by their armor, awkwardly made their way through the deadly attack to the shore.

Pigafetta recalled that Magellan, instead of rethinking the situation, ordered the men to do the one thing that was most likely to provoke the Mactanese: "Burn their houses in order to terrify them." Predictably, "when they saw their houses burning, they were roused to greater fury. . . . They came out of a path at the backs of our men, as if it had all been planned as an ambush, and, with earsplitting shouts, pounced on our men and began to kill them."

———

As the mayhem grew, the Europeans suffered more casualties. Even their armor failed to protect them against all the arrows flying in their direction. "So many of them charged down upon us that they shot the captain general through the right leg with a poisoned arrow." It was only now, too late, that Magellan realized the seriousness of his situation.

He finally gave the order to retreat, even though his men were stranded far from their longboats. More than forty of the Europeans scattered, while six or seven diehards, Pigafetta included, stuck by the wounded captain general: "The natives continued to pursue us, and picking up the same spear four or six times, hurled it at us again and again. Recognizing the captain general, so many turned on him that they knocked his helmet off his head twice, but he always stood firmly like a good knight, together with some others. Thus did we fight for one hour, refusing to retire farther."

All this time, no one came to the aid of Magellan and his small posse fighting for their lives—no Cebuans, and no reinforcements from the ships. Meanwhile, Magellan was rapidly weakening from the effects of the poisoned arrow in his leg. The Mactanese closed in, and the two sides fought hand to hand.

"Then, trying to lay his hand on sword, he could draw it out but halfway, because he had been wounded in the arm with a bamboo spear," Pigafetta wrote. "When the natives saw that, they all hurled themselves upon him. One of them wounded him on the left leg with a large cutlass." The wounded leader "turned back many times to see whether we were all in the boats," Pigafetta took care to note, and without that concern, "not a single one of us would have been saved in the boats, for while he was fighting, the others retired to the boats."

Repeated blows took their mortal toll on Magellan. "That caused the captain general to fall face downward, when immediately they rushed upon him with iron and bamboo spears and with their cutlasses, until they killed our mirror, our light, our comfort, and our true guide. Thereupon, beholding him dead, we, wounded, retreated as best we could to the boats, which were already pulling off."

At that moment, Sula's Cebuan warriors finally came to the Europeans' aid. They charged into the water, waving their swords, and drove off the Mactanese, who displayed little desire to make war on their neighbors. When the water had cleared, the Cebuans dragged the exhausted survivors into their *balanghais* and delivered them to the armada's longboats, which had remained curiously distant from the scene of battle.

This was not the dignified, religious ending that Magellan had imagined for himself in those pressured months of preparation in Seville three years before. No paupers would say prayers in his memory, no alms would be distributed in his name, no masses would be said for him in the churches of Seville. Nothing from his contested estate would go to his wife or young son. His illegitimate older son had been killed in battle at his side. Magellan would not be buried in the tranquil Seville cemetery he had picked out for himself. In short, none of the plans he had carefully set out in his will would come to pass. Instead, his body washed up on the sands of Mactan, where it was treated with utter indifference by the warriors who had defeated him.

————

In Magellan's death, Pigafetta, who had fought at his side, saw a shining example of nobility, heroism, and glorious acceptance of fate. In the most emotional entry of his entire diary, he memorialized his slain leader, whom he had revered: "I hope that . . . the fame of so noble a captain will not become effaced in our times. . . . And that his was the truth was seen openly, for no other had had so much natural talent nor the boldness to learn how to circumnavigate the world, as he had almost done." The word *almost* here was perhaps the saddest and most telling word in Pigafetta's eulogy.

"That battle was fought on Saturday, April 27, 1521," he concluded. "The captain general died on a Saturday because it was the day most holy to him. Eight of our men were killed with him, and four Indians who had become Christians and who had come afterward to aid us. . . . Of the enemy, only fifteen were killed, while many of us were wounded."

Pigafetta was genuinely devastated. He had left Europe as a young man of literary inclination, eager to explore the world as Magellan's guest, and now his captain general was dead, and who would be chosen as his successor was uncertain.

————

In death, Magellan was not a hero to everyone, not even to those who had admired his bravery and skill. His loyalists believed he had courted defeat by picking an unnecessary fight with the Mactanese. Magellan's gory demise was not the result of an unusual tactical error or a lapse of judgment. Rather, it was the direct outcome of Magellan's increasingly confrontational conduct in the Philippines. Through frequent displays of his military might, Magellan convinced the islanders—and himself—that he was invincible. It was only a matter of time until he provoked a confrontation with enemies who held a critical advantage, one from which faith alone could not protect him. In the end, the only peril he could not survive was the greatest of all: himself.

Magellan's death may also have been the result of one final mutiny by his own sailors. The whereabouts and actions of his backup are open to question—and to suspicion. From the standpoint of the men in the ships, this mutiny had the advantage of being easy to disguise; the revolt consisted of what they failed to do rather than what they did. Leaving Magellan to die the death of a thousand cuts in Mactan harbor, they allowed the Mactanese to do the dirty work for them.

After the furious battle ended that afternoon, Magellan's loyalists urged Humabon to send to Lapu Lapu a message requesting the remains of Magellan and the other victims of the battle of Mactan; they even offered to pay as much as the victors wanted in exchange for the bodies of the nine fallen soldiers.

Lapu Lapu's reply, recorded by Pigafetta, was blunt: "They would not give him for all the riches in the world. . . . They intended to keep him as a memorial." That might have been the case, and nothing of Magellan was ever recovered, not even his armor.

CHAPTER ELEVEN

— SHIP OF MUTINEERS —

T here was no discussion of disbanding the fleet or turning back. The Armada de Molucca had come too far and suffered too much for that. Nor was there any shortage of candidates to succeed Magellan. Although the loss of the captain general was tragic—no one, not even his critics, denied Magellan his courage—his death brought a sense of relief that the ordeal of sailing under him had at last ended.

The vote to select the next admiral resulted, oddly, in the election of not one but two men: Duarte Barbosa, Magellan's brother-in-law, and Juan Rodríguez Serrano, the Castilian captain. Even now, the sailors maintained a balance of power between the Spanish and Portuguese in the fleet.

Magellan's slave, Enrique, was bitterly opposed to the new leadership. Enrique had performed valuable service with his ability to interpret the Malay tongue, but he refused to leave *Trinidad*, claiming that he was suffering from battle wounds. He remained in his bunk, wrapped in a blanket, loudly announcing that he was free now that his master was dead. He was correct on this point; Magellan's will provided for Enrique's freedom along with a cash payment, but the new leaders of the expedition, still in need of his linguistic and diplomatic skills, insisted that he continue to obey orders. Enrique, after years of servitude, stubbornly refused to yield to Barbosa's authority—or anyone else's, for that matter.

Barbosa informed Enrique that "although his master was dead, he would not be set free or released, but that, when we reached Spain, he would still be the slave of Madame Beatriz, the wife of the deceased captain general." Serrano, elevating the argument even further, warned Enrique "that he would be whipped if he did not obey everything that he [Serrano] commanded." The two men's harsh words roused Enrique from his stupor, and he furiously stalked off the ship.

When Enrique left the ship, he found Cebu's king, Humabon. Enrique "told the Christian king that we were about to depart immediately"—this much was true—"and that, if he would follow his advice, he would gain all our ships and merchandise. And so they plotted a conspiracy. Then the slave returned to the ships, and he appeared to behave better than before."

Enrique's words had a drastic effect on Humabon, who found himself in a desperate situation. In the absence of the armada, Humabon had to contend with Lapu Lapu, who had been strengthened by his victory over Magellan. Because Humabon had sided with Magellan, it was only a matter of time until Lapu Lapu, seeking revenge, came after him. Pressure on Humabon to retaliate against the Europeans also came from another direction. Many of the island men resented the way their women had been treated by the Europeans. Plotting against Magellan's men was the most effective way for Humabon to demonstrate his loyalty to his own people and save his own neck.

————

On Wednesday, May 1, Humabon requested that the armada's leaders attend a feast. The invitation promised a lavish meal accompanied by gifts of jewels and other presents, which Humabon wished the fleet to carry across the waters as tribute to the king of Spain. The Christian king hoped that as many people as possible would enjoy his hospitality and generosity. Around thirty men, most of them officers, including Barbosa and Serrano, the new co-commanders, as well as their astronomer, Andrés de San Martín, decided to accept. Antonio Pigafetta was also invited to the feast, but he could not go because of the wound he had received at Magellan's side during the battle of Mactan.

Shortly after the officers went ashore, "we heard great cries and groans," said Pigafetta. "Then we quickly raised the anchors, and, firing several pieces of artillery at their houses, we approached nearer to shore." What they saw exceeded their worst nightmare:

As the banquet was about to end, some armed people emerged from the palm grove and attacked the invitees, killing twenty-seven of them, and captured the priest who had remained there and Juan Serrano, the pilot, who was an old man; others . . . swam to the ships and, helped by those aboard, cut the cables and set sail; the barbarians . . . brought Juan Serrano to the shore and said that they wanted to exchange him for ransom. The old man implored our men with words and tears to feel sympathy for his old age. . . .

Our men told him that they would do as they could. The ransom was discussed and they asked for an iron gun, which is what they fear the most. . . . No sooner would our men grant their request than the Indians would reply asking for more, and this continued until, realizing their intention, those aboard the ships did not want to remain there any longer and said to Juan Serrano that he himself could very well see what was going on, and how the Indians' words were all but a pretence.

Serrano pleaded for his crew members to come to his rescue, but his friend João Lopes Carvalho refused to intervene. Pigafetta was appalled by this cowardice, but there was nothing he could do. Stranded on the shore, Serrano confirmed that the other men, including Barbosa and San Martín, were dead, slaughtered during Humabon's banquet. Left behind, Serrano was eventually killed. Enrique's revenge on the Europeans had been bloodier than anyone could have foreseen.

The three black ships of the Armada de Molucca raised anchor, set sail, and headed out of Cebu harbor with all the speed they could muster. Only 115 men remained of the 260 who had left Spain, and as they fled to safety, their last sight of Cebu was of the islanders tearing down the cross on the mountaintop and smashing it to bits.

———

Five days later, and half a world away, a weather-beaten vessel tied up at the harbor in Seville. The arrival of a ship from distant lands was hardly an unusual event in Seville, but she was not just any vessel, this was *San Antonio*, part of the Armada de Molucca. It was Monday, May 6, 1521, and the event marked the first that had been heard of the fleet since it had left Sanlúcar de Barrameda on September 20, 1519.

No one ashore knew what to make of her arrival; the fleet had not been expected to return for another year. They would soon learn that Magellan had found the mythical strait but that *San Antonio* had been hijacked by mutineers. She carried her captain, Estêvão Gomes; his chief co-conspirator, Gerónimo Guerra; and fifty-five other men, including Magellan's cousin Álvaro de Mesquita, whom the mutineers had kept in irons throughout the return journey.

Under Guerra's command, Gomes had skillfully piloted the ship across the Atlantic to Spain. Despite having braved the Atlantic Ocean alone, *San Antonio*'s captain and crew felt no joy on seeing Seville's familiar cathedral because they were returning as mutineers who faced the prospect of an official inquiry, incarceration, and even punishment by death.

They expected to draw strength from Magellan's lack of popularity in Spain and planned to destroy the Portuguese captain general's reputation with tales of his poor judgment and brutal mistreatment of Spanish officers. But their stories had to be compelling, because their lives depended on convincing the authorities that the mutiny had been necessary and justified. Of course, Magellan would not be present to plead his case. The only one likely to speak up on his behalf was Álvaro de Mesquita, whose wounds offered evidence of the mutineers' tactics. And Mesquita had used the long sea journey home to prepare for an inquiry, because his life also depended on how persuasively he argued his case.

———

The moment King Charles heard that *San Antonio* had returned, he ordered the Casa de Contratación to sell anything of value aboard the

124

ship and hand over anything over ten thousand ducats to the crown. The young king was eager to get his hands on the money, if there was any.

As it happened, there was none. The Casa's detailed inventory of the ship's contents included tarnished combs, crumbling paper, rusty knives, scissors, and bent sewing needles, but no spices—nothing, in fact, of any great value. Furthermore, the ship was in bad shape after eighteen months at sea. The authorities in Seville quickly realized that *San Antonio* had not made it to the Spice Islands. No one aboard knew what had happened to Magellan. The *San Antonio* and her mutinous, ragtag crew were presumed to be the only survivors of what had once been the glorious Armada de Molucca. The king's dreams of claiming the Moluccas for the glory of Spain would have to wait.

———

Within days of their return, the mutineers delivered their finely crafted accounts to the Casa de Contratación. Fifty-three out of the fifty-five crew members gave depositions, and the sudden activity threw the Casa's clerks into a frenzy.

Mesquita, meanwhile, went directly from confinement aboard ship to jail on land. The Casa's representatives insisted they were only protecting Mesquita from the others, but the overthrown captain believed he had been singled out for unfair treatment.

The Casa did a remarkably thorough job in uncovering the details of the mutiny at the strait. As the report unfolded, a strong anti-Magellan bias became increasingly clear. Not surprisingly, the mutineers rearranged events at Port Saint Julian to suit their cause. To hear them tell it, they made Magellan furious by simply asking him to obey the king's orders, or at least their interpretation of them.

The mutineers overlooked Magellan's successful effort to sabotage the revolt by sending a sailor to sever a cable tying up *San Antonio*. In their account, Cartagena and Quesada ordered the rebel ships to sail out of Port Saint Julian, an act that meant confronting Magellan, whose flagship, *Trinidad*, blocked their path to freedom. The mutineers invented still more incidents with Mesquita playing a critical part.

For example, as the rebel ships sailed past the flagship, Mesquita was supposed to ask Magellan not to fire on them so they could "iron out their differences, but before they could move from where they were, in the middle of the night while the men slept, the flagship fired heavy and light volleys at their ship." This was a good story, but the truth was that *San Antonio*, carried along by a powerful current and dragging its anchor, had approached *Trinidad* because its cable had parted, not because Quesada had given the order to sail.

Not surprisingly, the mutineers colored the climactic revolt at the strait in their favor. In their version, Mesquita provoked the rebellion by stabbing Gomes in the leg, and Gomes retaliated by stabbing Mesquita's left hand. (In reality, of course, Gomes had stabbed Mesquita first.) They also insisted that the trip home had been unspeakably difficult because each man was limited to a ration of three ounces of bread a day. This was another obvious fib, because *San Antonio* carried provisions for the entire fleet, more than enough food to fill the mutineers' bellies.

In their depositions, the crew members skillfully played on Spanish fears that Magellan was a Portuguese tyrant: a cunning agent of his native land who assembled the Armada de Molucca at Spain's expense merely to destroy it and to deceive King Charles. Magellan was a murderer who tortured honorable Spanish officers with connections in the highest possible place, the Church. They told the tragic tale of Cartagena—a Castilian officer!—whom Magellan left to rot on a remote island. As if that were not wicked enough, the captain general left a priest to the same miserable fate.

While the mutineers spun their tales for the Casa's representatives, Gomes and Guerra were held in custody, as was Mesquita, despite his claims that he was the mutiny's principal victim, not its perpetrator. From his jail cell, Mesquita insisted, truthfully, that he had been tortured into signing the confession, that it was false, and that he had acted loyally to Magellan and the king of Spain. In his defense, he presented the Casa with the documents he had kept during the mutiny trial in Port Saint Julian, recording the rebellious actions of every accused crew member.

Mesquita's account, so different from the mutineers' twisted version, received little attention and even less credibility at the Casa de Contratación. He was ordered to remain in prison. While the mutiny's ringleaders, Gomes and Guerra, had their travel expenses to and from court reimbursed, Mesquita, considered guilty until proven otherwise, was ordered to pay the costs of his trial out of his own tattered pocket.

———————

On May 26, Archbishop Fonseca—Cartagena's father—delivered his response to the depositions. The mutineers' conspiracy to distort the truth worked more or less as planned. Fonseca expressed shock and dismay at Magellan's treatment of Cartagena and Quesada. It seemed incredible that Spanish officers would be capable of mutiny. So the mutineers went free, though a hint of suspicion clung to them and they did not receive the back pay they claimed was due them.

In Magellan's absence, his wife, Beatriz, became an object of suspicion, as if she had involved herself with events at the other end of the world. The Casa de Contratación cut off her financial resources and ordered Beatriz and their young son to be placed under house arrest; they were forbidden to return to Portugal while the inquiry continued. Of course, she had no way of knowing that her husband had died only weeks before, on April 27, in the battle of Mactan, followed by her brother, Duarte Barbosa, who died in the massacre at Cebu.

But Fonseca was almost as suspicious of the mutineers as he was of Magellan loyalists. He ordered Gomes, Guerra, and several other ringleaders to be brought to him in custody, insisting that they travel separately because they might continue to conspire. No one besides Mesquita spoke up on Magellan's behalf. Mesquita, whose chief crime was being Magellan's cousin, remained confined in jail.

———————

The inquiry into the mutiny on *San Antonio* consumed six months, and in the end Guerra and Gomes were set free along with all the sailors; Gomes even received a royal appointment to another expedition.

Those who sided with Magellan fared much worse. His wife and son remained under house arrest, and now his father-in-law, the well-connected and prominent Diogo Barbosa, was ordered to hand over property that Magellan had given to him before the fleet left Seville. This shabby treatment made Barbosa furious, and he spoke to the king in defense of Magellan's conduct during the mutiny. Barbosa recklessly lectured King Charles about the principles at stake: "These [events] serve as bad examples which discourage those who wish to do what they should and give greater encouragement to those who do otherwise." Yet Barbosa's passionate arguments backfired. As a Portuguese, Barbosa was seen as treasonous rather than honorable, and his star fell along with Magellan's.

———

Seville, the center of Spanish commerce, developed a reputation as a city in crisis. Criminal behavior flourished in its streets and alleys and shabbier neighborhoods. Triana, the suburb across the Guadalquivir River, served as home to many underworld types, as well as to slaves and the sailors who manned Spanish ships. Gypsies, palm readers, beggars, itinerant actors, and minstrels populated a rapidly expanding underworld.

With goods flowing into Seville from Africa and across Europe, smuggling became a major enterprise; the value of smuggled goods exceeded that of legitimate merchandise. Meanwhile, Seville's wealthy nobles, with their impressive castles, were renowned and envied across Spain.

These two opposing sides of Seville met at the docks, where wealthy merchants met sailors and dishonest middlemen seeking merchandise to sell. Amid the chaos on the banks of the Guadalquivir, *San Antonio*, now stripped of her rigging and fittings, rode at anchor, a silent witness to an expedition gone wrong.

In Seville, no one yet knew that the Armada de Molucca had successfully navigated the strait and crossed the immense Pacific Ocean. No one realized how close the survivors were to their ultimate goal, the Spice Islands. Everyone—from King Charles to the bureaucrats in the Casa de Contratación to the recently freed sailors looking for their next ship—assumed that the fleet was lost and the expedition a complete failure.

Everyone was wrong.

CHAPTER TWELVE

SURVIVORS

T en thousand miles from Spain, in a remote corner of the Philippine archipelago, a ship was burning. The blaze turned night into day, and its reflection formed hypnotic patterns on the inky, swelling sea.

The ship was *Concepción*, one of the three vessels that had escaped the massacre at Cebu the previous day. Since then, the 115 survivors had tried to navigate the three large vessels around the uncharted shoals and islands of the Philippines, but they soon discovered that they were hopelessly shorthanded. To add to their problems, shipworms had infested the hull. Magellan, had he been alive, would have ordered the men to undertake grueling repairs, but the survivors adopted a more practical approach and decided to burn the ship to prevent it from falling into the hands of an enemy who might use it against them. The crew transferred the contents of *Concepción*—her provisions, rigging, sails, fittings, weapons, and navigational devices—to the two other ships, *Trinidad*, still the flagship of the fleet, and *Victoria*. And then, on the night of May 2, 1521, the empty ship was set on fire.

A quick vote among the sailors placed Gonzalo Gómez de Espinosa, the *alguacil*, in command of *Victoria*, while João Lopes Carvalho, the Portuguese pilot, won election as the new captain general—the fourth man to hold that office since the fleet had left Seville. Juan Sebastián Elcano, now the master of *Victoria*, silently cursed the new captain general, who might have been a talented pilot but was incapable of disciplining the unruly fleet. In Brazil, Carvalho had attempted to bring his mistress on board; although he did not succeed, their child had been traveling with the fleet ever since.

Elcano had no respect for a leader who set such a poor example for the others.

After the multiple tragedies the armada had suffered in the Philippines, commercial goals ruled their actions. Never again would their ships sail into a peaceful harbor and insist on mass conversions. Knowing they were lucky to be alive, the men turned their attention to reaching the Spice Islands, where they hoped to find safety, supplies, and the precious commodity they had sailed halfway around the world to find.

Carvalho faced the task of leading the fleet's two remaining ships southward through the archipelago to the Moluccas, but the arrival of the rainy season and its storms in the Philippines often made navigation next to impossible. For the short distances and intricate maneuvering involved, the sailors needed a reliable map or, at least, a guide familiar with these waters, but after their horrific experiences on Cebu and Mactan, they were reluctant to ask for help.

Occasionally, the fleet was approached by large proas powered by rowers chanting in unison. Whenever possible, Pigafetta asked the rowers for directions to the Moluccas, but otherwise the fleet kept their relations with the islanders to a bare minimum.

———

Carvalho, aided by Francisco Albo, the pilot, veered from one island to another, following a winding but generally southerly course through the labyrinth of the Philippine archipelago. They were veering seriously off course, heading west into the Sulu Sea, toward China, rather than south to the Spice Islands.

The search for food grew more frantic. "We were often on the point of abandoning the ships in order that we might not die of hunger," Pigafetta wrote. At last they arrived at "the land of promise, because we suffered great hunger before we found it." The island was called Palawan, and it divides the Sulu Sea and the South China Sea.

Their stomachs growling and their heads spinning from fatigue and hunger, the sailors rushed through another *casicasi* ceremony with the local chieftain and then gorged themselves with "rice, ginger, swine, goats, fowls," and "figs . . . as thick as the arm." Pigafetta declared these "figs," actually bananas, to be "excellent" food.

Pigafetta charmed his island hosts into displaying their exotic weapons for him: "They have blowpipes with thick wooden arrows more than one *palmo* [handspan] long, with harpoon points, and others tipped with fishbones, and poisoned with an herb."

————

When the crew had rested and loaded provisions onto the ships, they weighed anchor, and on June 21, 1521, prepared to leave Palawan. Carvalho ordered the fleet to encircle a large proa. Pretending to have peaceful intentions, the armada instead captured all three of the pilots, believing that they would lead the way to the Spice Islands at last, but these pilots—all Arabs—complicated matters by directing the Armada southwest, toward Brunei, an Arab stronghold, rather than southeast, toward the Moluccas.

This was a hazardous crossing, filled with shoals and sandbanks. At last, on July 8, they dropped anchor in the harbor of Brunei, in the midst of a realm of luxury that would surpass anything they had previously experienced on the voyage.

The next day what appeared to be a proa approached the ships, but this was not the same rough craft skimming across the water. It was a much larger vessel "whose bow and stern were worked in gold. At the bow flew a white and blue banner surmounted with peacock feathers." Trailing the proa were two smaller vessels. To add to the theatrical nature of the scene, musicians on board serenaded the shocked Europeans. "Some of the men were playing on musical instruments and drums," Pigafetta noted in disbelief.

The proa's crew signaled that they wished to board, and "eight old men, who were chiefs, entered the ships and took seats in the stern upon a carpet. They presented us with a painted wooden jar full of betel and areca (the fruit which they chew continually), and jasmine." The old chiefs brought much more: bolts of yellow silk cloth, two cages filled with flapping fowl, jars filled with rice wine, and bundles of sugarcane. After delivering their offerings aboard *Trinidad*, the chiefs did the same with *Victoria*.

Their generosity likely stemmed from a case of mistaken identity. Most of these regions had been visited by the Portuguese, who, traveling a different route, had pioneered trading relationships with the local rulers. That made the Armada de Molucca an impostor, but many of the crew were Portuguese and appeared to be the latest representatives of the Portuguese crown.

———

The fleet remained anchored off Brunei for six peaceful days, allowing the men to recover, at least partially, from the last few weeks. From the decks of their ships, the men could see an assortment of elevated houses constructed over a complicated series of waterways, piers, and boardwalks.

The fleet's isolation ended when they were approached by a group of proas. Arriving "with great pomp," Pigafetta wrote, the proas "encircled the ships with musical instruments playing and drums and brass gongs beating. They saluted us with their peculiar cloth caps which cover only the top of their heads. We saluted them by firing our mortars without stones [bullets]. Then they gave us a present of various kinds of food, made only of rice. . . . They told us that their king was willing to let us get water and wood, and to trade at our pleasure."

The messenger from the king, or sultan, of Brunei promised to help them with all their needs. He wanted to know where they were going, and when they spoke of the Moluccas, he said there was nothing there but cloves. However, if they were determined to go, he would supply a pilot for each ship. After months in tropical water, the hulls badly needed reconditioning. The messenger explained that sailors from Brunei "caulked their own boats with a pitch they made with coconut oil and wax, for which they could send out some people to town, where they could find many things to buy." And again he invited the men to stay awhile and sample the pleasures of Brunei.

The crew members sent Espinosa, Elcano, two Greek sailors, Carvalho's Brazilian son, Pigafetta, and one other sailor. The group boarded the golden proa, bearing gifts salvaged from the wreckage of the fleet. After a short trip over water, they reached an elaborate city "entirely built in salt water," said Pigafetta, "except the houses of the king and certain chiefs. It contains twenty-five thousand fires"—that is to say hearths, indicating family units. "There is a large brick wall in front of the king's house with towers like a fort, in which were mounted fifty-six bronze pieces, and six of iron." The gunpowder for these weapons was likely imported from China, where it had been invented. After months of drifting among more primitive tribes, the sailors had reached a civilization at least as advanced as their own.

After waiting in the proa for two hours, Pigafetta, Elcano, and the others were invited to mount elephants, and from their swaying seats they surveyed the landscape. Reaching their destination, the elephants kneeled, discharging their astonished passengers, who immediately sat down to a great feast. After they ate and drank their way into a state of pleasant confusion, they were treated to "cotton mattresses, whose lining was of taffeta and the sheets of Cambaia." It was the first night the men had slept on mattresses and linen since they had left Seville.

––––––––

At noon the next day, the men remounted the elephants and proceeded to the sultan's palace while onlookers treated them with a respect reserved for great dignitaries. Dismounting, they passed through a courtyard to a "large hall full of many nobles," perhaps as many as three hundred, and came upon an extraordinary scene: "We sat down upon a carpet with the presents in the jars near us. At the end of the small hall was a large window from which a brocade curtain was drawn aside so that we could see within it the king seated at a table with one of his young sons, chewing betel. No one but women were behind him."

They were cautioned not to speak directly to the sultan. Should they wish to say anything, they were to inform a servant, who would pass it on to an official of slightly higher rank, who would then tell the governor's brother, who would whisper the message through a "speaking-tube" passing through the wall, where another servant would intercept it and relay it to the sultan. As if that were not sufficiently off-putting, they were instructed to kowtow before the sultan: "The chief taught us the manner of making three obeisances to the king with our hands clasped above the head, raising first one foot and then the other and then kissing the hands toward him, and we did so, that being the method of the royal obeisance."

Once they had completed the formalities, Pigafetta explained that they wished only to make peace and to trade. The sultan happily cooperated. Take water and wood, he offered, and trade as you wish. Of greater importance, the sultan offered samples of cinnamon and cloves, the spices his guests had been seeking for nearly two years. It appeared they were now on the Spice Islands' doorstep.

After the audience, the Europeans were ceremoniously returned atop elephants to the governor's house, accompanied by seven bearers carrying the presents. That evening, Pigafetta claimed they dined on thirty-two different kinds of meat, in addition to the fish. Even then, nearly a century after the era of the Treasure Fleet, Chinese wares were everywhere. Pigafetta mentioned porcelain ("a kind of very white earthenware"); silk; and, amazingly enough, "iron spectacles."

After their second night ashore, Pigafetta and one sailor rode by elephant back to the ocean and boarded their crude and confined ships. Elcano, Espinosa, the two Greek sailors, and Carvalho's son remained ashore. The Europeans, suspecting the missing were being held hostage against their will, anxiously waited for their safe return.

———

Shortly after dawn on July 29, more than one hundred proas, organized into three groups, appeared out of nowhere. To complicate matters, two great junks had anchored just behind the armada during the night. No one aboard *Trinidad* or *Victoria* noticed the junks at the time, but it now appeared that the proas intended to drive the armada toward the junks, whose crew would overwhelm the Europeans and take them as prisoners, or worse.

Fearing for their lives, the crew decided to fight. Some crew members jumped aboard the junks and captured four warriors. The men-at-arms fired their weapons at their adversaries, "killing many persons," according to Pigafetta. Several of the proas, their occupants frightened by the armada's response, veered away. Nevertheless, the battle raged on, as the armada turned its guns on one of the huge junks. The Europeans swarmed the junk, where they discovered that its captain was not the murderous pirate they had imagined.

"Their captain said that he served the king of Luzon and that while with a fleet to an island he had been cut off from the rest of the ships by a storm," Pigafetta explained. Carvalho and the captain fell into secret conversation, to the shock of the armada's officers who had risked their lives to board the junk. In hushed tones, the captain offered Carvalho jewels, two cutlasses, and a dagger "with many diamonds," all for his personal use. The gifts had their intended effect: "Our captain released the junk and its people, something which everyone later regretted because they saw that under their poor-looking cotton garments, most of those men were wearing silk clothes with gold embroidery."

Pigafetta recognized the transaction as a simple case of bribery, and his opinion of Carvalho, never high to begin with, fell several notches. Had they held the admiral hostage, Pigafetta believed, the sultan of Brunei would have paid a tremendous ransom for him, far more than the bribe that Carvalho had accepted.

The matter did not end there. The sultan revealed that the men in the proas had had no intention of attacking the armada. They actually had been on their way to do battle with the sultan's enemies aboard the junks when the armada got in the way and ruined their battle plan. Once they realized their mistake, the armada's officers awkwardly struggled to make amends with the sultan and requested that the detained men, including Carvalho's son, be returned. But the sultan refused. After being pampered, the Europeans had repaid his generosity by meddling in his internal affairs and letting the admiral go. As a result, he insisted on holding his hostages.

Carvalho responded with an insult of his own. He decided to keep the warriors he had captured at sea, as well as another prize: three extraordinarily beautiful women. He declared that he would present them to King Charles, a plan that the other officers enthusiastically seconded. Magellan had always forbidden women aboard the ships because he believed their presence would cause trouble, and he was right. Soon everyone on board *Trinidad* was aware that Carvalho had turned the women into his personal harem.

————————

Eventually, the sultan of Brunei released two hostages, Elcano and Espinosa. They said they had been detained separately and treated well. But where were the others? Elcano and Espinosa explained that the two Greek sailors had decided to desert. The story seemed unlikely, but there was no way to confirm it. Magellan, had he been alive, would have immediately searched for the deserters, but Carvalho did not lift a finger. He was naturally more interested in the fate of his young son. With long faces, Elcano and Espinosa said they had heard the boy had died ashore, but they did not know for certain.

That was only the beginning of Carvalho's misfortunes. On September 21, 1521, the other officers decided to replace him. The change of command was not a mutiny, and Carvalho was simply told to step down. He did so, returning to his former post as *Trinidad*'s pilot.

The officers settled on an awkward lineup to command the fleet. Martín Méndez, the purser (the officer in charge of money matters), became the fifth captain general, and Gonzalo Gómez de Espinosa, the *alguacil*, took over the captaincy of *Trinidad*, still the flagship. Elcano gnashed his teeth in frustration, having been passed over for captain general yet again. Still, he could console himself with becoming the captain of *Victoria*. And because neither Espinosa nor Méndez had firsthand navigation experience, Elcano, with long experience as a pilot, became the unofficial head of the expedition.

After thirty-five days in Brunei, the fleet was finally ready to depart for the Moluccas. But both ships leaked rapidly, and it became apparent to all that they would have to recondition them. Arriving on the island of Cimbonbon, the armada spent the next forty-two days on repairs.

Once the grueling renovations were completed, the fleet resumed its search for the Spice Islands on September 27. Traveling southeast, they arrived at another island in the vicinity of Mindanao that Pigafetta called Monoripa. "The people of that island make their dwellings in boats and do not live otherwise," he observed of the Bajau, the sea nomads who were widely scattered throughout the area, adjusting their moorings to avoid the monsoon.

Just before they left, they got their first, tantalizing look at the nearly mythical cinnamon tree: "It has but three or four small branches and its leaves resemble those of the laurel. Its bark is the cinnamon, and it is gathered twice a year." The men conducted a quick, probably underhanded transaction, exchanging two large knives for seventeen libras of cinnamon, worth enough on the docks of Seville to buy an entire ship. (The libra was a unit of weight; its abbreviation, *lb*, is still used for pounds today.) They expected to get far more cinnamon— along with nutmeg, pepper, mace, and many other precious spices— once they reached their goal.

Desperate to reach the Spice Islands, they attacked a large proa to learn their whereabouts. In a bitter struggle, they killed seven of the eighteen men on board the little craft. Among those spared was the brother of Mindanao's ruler, who insisted that he knew the way to the Moluccas.

Changing course, the sailor from Mindanao took them to the southeast. Along the way, they passed a cape inhabited by cannibals, whom Pigafetta described as "shaggy men who are exceedingly great fighters and archers"; he explained, "They use swords one *palmo* in length and eat only raw human hearts with the juice of oranges and lemons." The crew members naturally kept their distance and listened closely to their captured guide's account of the tribe.

On the ships sailed, gliding past the islands of Sanguir, Kima, Karakitang, Para, Sarangalong, Siao, Tagulanda, Zoar, Meau, Paginsara, Suar, and Atean: a string of emeralds set in gleaming sapphire. And then, on November 6, 1521, they saw four more islands shimmering on the horizon. "The pilot who still remained with us told us that those four islands were the Moluccas," Pigafetta recorded. After losing three ships and over a hundred men—more than half the crew—they were finally on the doorstep of the Spice Islands.

To Europeans of the sixteenth century, the term *Moluccas* referred to just five islands. Four of them, each no more than six miles across, stretched from north to south: Ternate, Tidore, Motil, and Maquian. To the south lay the fifth, Bacan, which was considerably larger. The best-known among them were Ternate and Tidore, volcanic islands that towered about a mile above the sea. Volcanic ash enriched the soil on the islands where the spices grew, and the climate promoted lush growth; this combination made them unique sources for spices. The occasional volcanic eruptions gave them a magical reputation. It would not have been more marvelous to see a dragon or the lost city of Atlantis rising from the depths of the sea than to witness an eruption in the Moluccas.

The destination was now within the grasp of the Armada de Molucca. "So we thanked God, and for joy we discharged all our artillery," Pigafetta wrote. "And no wonder we were so joyful, for we had spent twenty-seven months less two days in our search for the Moluccas."

CHAPTER THIRTEEN
ARRIVAL IN
PARADISE

On November 8, 1521, the Armada de Molucca entered the harbor of Tidore, firing a joyful salute. In the humid climate, the strong scents of cloves and cinnamon wafted across the water, reviving the crew members with the promise of riches.

The following day, the ruler of Tidore floated out to the ships in a luxurious proa. His head was protected from the sun by a silk awning; his son, holding a ceremonial scepter, was at his side. He was accompanied by a pair of ritual hand washers carrying sweet water in jars made of gold, and two others carrying a gold casket filled with betel nuts. He introduced himself as al-Mansur, a Muslim name, but the officers came to know him by the Spanish version, Almanzor.

From his magnificent proa, Almanzor enthusiastically welcomed the fleet. "After such long tossing upon the seas, and so many dangers, come and enjoy the pleasures of the land, and refresh your bodies, and do not think but that you have arrived at the kingdom of your own sovereign," he stated, according to Pigafetta. And then Almanzor stunned them all by announcing that he had dreamed of their arrival, and they had fulfilled his prophecy.

Almanzor boarded *Trinidad* under the watchful eyes of the officers, who offered him a velvet-covered chair of honor. Almanzor said he was familiar with Spain, and even with its great and powerful ruler, King Charles. He insisted that he and the people of Tidore deeply desired to serve the king and his kingdom.

Obtaining Almanzor's goodwill was essential; he was, after all, the gatekeeper to the cloves. But Almanzor's little kingdom was in constant danger, and he needed these visitors from afar as much as they needed him and his spices. A decade earlier, his father had encouraged the Portuguese to set up a trading station because he wished to undo the Arab monopoly on the islands' crops. The experience had left a bitter legacy on both sides. The Portuguese came to detest the Moluccans with passion. The islanders turned out to be untrustworthy partners; they continued to sell spices to anyone who brought a ship capable of carrying them away. As a result, Portugal never achieved total dominance in the Spice Islands.

Almanzor had grown tired of the Portuguese and wanted to switch allegiance to the Spaniards (although he did not realize that many of the armada's crew were Portuguese). But there was more: local politics. At the time, Tidore was in the midst of a conflict with its island neighbor, Ternate, still in the Portuguese grip, and Almanzor thought these representatives of the Spanish crown could make powerful allies in the struggle.

———————

On November 10, Carvalho and a small group went ashore, and for the first time the men of the Armada de Molucca set foot on the Spice Islands.

The armada's men had seen cloves, smelled cloves, and tasted cloves, but only now did they find cloves growing in the wild—not just a few trees scattered here and there, but a dense forest.

The armada's leaders reached an agreement with Almanzor recognizing Spain's sovereignty over the island, even though the agreement violated the Treaty of Tordesillas. Once these formalities were over, the sailors pushed to obtain the spices as quickly as they could, before an outbreak of local conflict could drive them away.

The king of Tidore told the armada's officers that he did not have enough cloves on hand to satisfy their needs, but he offered to accompany them to Bacan, where he assured them they could find as much as they could want. Before the officers began filling the ships with spices, they wanted to know what had become of one of their own: Francisco Serrão, the author of the letters that had inspired

Magellan's voyage. It was possible that Serrão was still in the Spice Islands, and, if so, the armada's officers hoped to reunite with him.

The reunion was not to be. Almanzor explained that Serrão had died eight months earlier, about the time of Magellan's death. But the king concealed the whole story behind Serrão's end. After his arrival in the Spice Islands in 1512, Serrão had chosen sides in a power struggle between the rulers of Tidore and Ternate and had served as admiral of the Ternate navy. The two island kingdoms battled for years, with Ternate, under Serrão's leadership, winning every time. To make peace, Serrão forced Tidore to give up the sons of its rulers as hostages and forced Almanzor to marry off his daughter to his enemy, the king of Ternate, whose child she had. Almanzor neither forgot nor forgave the terrible humiliations Serrão had inflicted on him, and when Serrão came to Tidore to trade cloves, Almanzor had him poisoned.

Serrão's death echoed Magellan's. Each had taken sides in a struggle between two island kingdoms, and each had acted harshly toward the enemy. Eventually, the outsider paid for his actions with his life.

———

On Monday, November 11, one of the king of Ternate's many sons approached the fleet in a proa, accompanied by Serrão's widow, who was a Javanese woman, and their two children.

Espinosa and the other officers aboard *Trinidad* welcomed the visitors, gave them gifts, and watched closely for signs of trouble. Meanwhile, Pigafetta chatted with a servant named Manuel, who served a Portuguese sailor, Pedro Afonso de Lorosa, who had come to the Spice Islands with Serrão and still lived there. Manuel claimed that the rulers of Ternate were also in favor of Spain, and he assured the officers that they were as welcome on Ternate as they were on Tidore.

Meanwhile, trading for spices got under way with astonishing speed. By Tuesday, November 12, four days after dropping anchor in Tidore harbor, the Armada de Molucca was in business. "We immediately began to trade in the following manner. For ten brazas of red cloth of

142

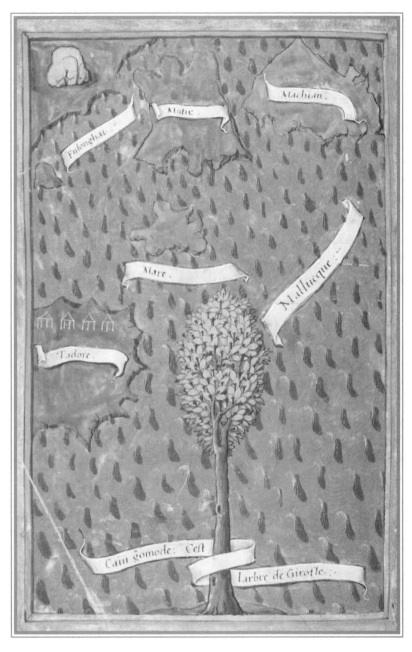

Tidore and the other Spice Islands depicted with a clove tree in an illustration from Pigafetta's journal.

very good quality, they gave us one bahar of cloves, which is equivalent to four quintals and six libras." A quintal of cloves equaled a hundred pounds, and it was the most important unit for measuring the value of a spice shipment. The men of the armada traded the gongs, knives, and other items pirated from the Chinese junks they had raided en route for the cloves. In return for these trinkets, they received a haul that a sailor might expect to see only once or twice in a lifetime.

As trading proceeded, Almanzor did all he could to put the armada at ease, even when the officers revealed that they were holding sixteen captives, taken from islands they had visited. To the officers' surprise, the confession delighted the king, and he asked to take possession of the captives "so that he might send them back to their land with five of his own men that they might make the king of Spain and his fame known." There was also the ticklish matter of Carvalho's harem of three captive women, whom the officers delivered to Almanzor.

———————

On the afternoon of November 13, Pedro Afonso de Lorosa, Francisco Serrão's companion, signaled the fleet from a proa. He excitedly explained that the king of Ternate had given him permission for the visit and instructed him to answer all questions truthfully, adding jokingly, "even if he did come from Ternate." What followed was one of the more remarkable meetings in the Age of Discovery. In a time when travelers who had become separated from their native cultures were often never heard from again, here was a Portuguese explorer standing before the Spanish armada's officers after a ten-year silence, in good humor and eager to share vital intelligence.

The officers learned that "one year less fifteen days ago a great ship from Malacca had come there and left with a cargo of cloves" and that this ship was looking for the armada. Lorosa ended his tale with a bombshell: "The king of Portugal had already secretly enjoyed Molucca for ten years, [and] the King of Spain should not know."

This piece of information explained why King Manuel had refused

A Portuguese pilot's chart of the Spice Islands dating from 1519. Such charts were prized—and closely guarded—in the Age of Discovery.

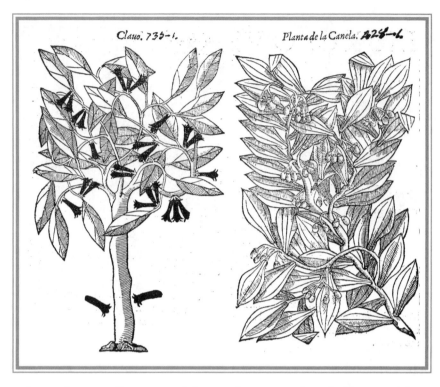

Sixteenth-century illustrations of cloves and cinnamon, from the Treatise of the Drugs and Medicines of the East Indies *by Cristobal Acosta, published in 1579.*

Magellan four times: Portuguese ships were already trading in the Spice Islands, and a water route such as the one Magellan proposed threatened to disturb Portugal's secret spice trade. Spain, with no such secret relationship, would naturally benefit from Magellan's plan.

Not until three o'clock in the morning did the exhausted wanderer reach the end of his tale. Amazed by his stories, the officers begged him to join them, "promising him good wages and salaries." Lorosa, a man without a country, agreed. He would come to regret this decision.

———

On November 15, Almanzor went to Bacan to gather cloves for the Portuguese. Later that day, Pigafetta finally had his chance to examine cloves firsthand. These aromatic bushes had inspired the voyage that had cost so many lives, moved the destinies of empire around the world, and laid the foundation for an emerging world economy. Centuries before Magellan, the Chinese had imported cloves, which were believed to have medical properties and were also used to flavor food and to sweeten breath. Europe found even more applications for the clove. Its essence, when applied to the eyes, supposedly improved vision. Its powder, when applied to the forehead, supposedly relieved fevers and colds. It was miraculous, precious, and wonderful. Pigafetta wrote:

> No cloves are grown in the world except in the five mountains of those five islands. . . . Almost every day we saw a mist descend and encircle now one and now another of those mountains, on account of which those cloves become perfect. Each of those people possesses clove trees, and each one watches over his own trees although he does not cultivate them.

In the early hours of Monday, November 25, Almanzor sailed out to the fleet in his proa to announce the cloves would be ready for delivery in four days. Overjoyed, the men of the armada fired their weapons to celebrate and to impress the king. Later the same day, the men began to load what eventually amounted to about a thousand pounds. The more spices they took on board, the more anxious the men became to return to Spain before another disaster unfolded.

———

Now that the Europeans finally had their hands on the spices, Almanzor sought to involve them in local politics, explaining that he wanted his visitors to return to the islands as soon as possible with even more ships to "avenge the murder of his father." Even though the officers had experienced the bitter lessons of becoming involved in local battles, they assured the king that they would help him. Content with this vague promise of assistance, the king invited everyone ashore for a banquet to celebrate the occasion.

The innocent gesture immediately sent the men of the armada into a panic because it reminded them of both the massacre at the banquet on Cebu and of Serrão's death by poisoning. Suddenly, the officers saw signs of impending doom wherever they looked. They instead invited Almanzor to board *Trinidad*. The king accepted and was "greatly amazed" to hear that the armada was about to weigh anchor and sail away. He meant no harm, he said, and only wanted to help them obtain their spices and journey home safely. He demonstrated his sincerity by saying that if the armada wanted to leave now, he would do nothing to stop them; he requested only that they take back all their gifts "because the kings his neighbors would say that the king of Tidore had received so many gifts from so great a king"—that is, King Charles—"and had given him nothing, and they would think that we had departed only for fear of some deception and treachery, whereby he would always be named and reputed a traitor," Pigafetta wrote.

So here was the reason Almanzor wanted the armada to stay: If he could maintain an alliance with his powerful visitors, he would impress and intimidate the jealous rulers of the other islands, but if he lost the visitors' favor, if they dismissed him as insignificant, he would appear vulnerable to the rival kings. The loss of face could cost him his kingdom, or even his life.

The king's appeal softened the officers' hearts, and they decided to stay another fifteen days. To strengthen their shared bond of loyalty to the king of Spain, the officers gave the grateful king a royal banner displaying the insignia associated with King Charles.

————

Working feverishly throughout the last days of November and the early days of December, the men of the Armada de Molucca purchased and stored cloves until they had no more caps, bells, mirrors, hatchets, scissors, bolts of cloth, or other trinkets to exchange, and no more room to store the aromatic treasure.

On the designated day of departure, the kings of all the Spice Islands assembled to see the fleet off. The ships' gunner fired their artillery one more time, but in the midst of the excitement, *Trinidad's* cables failed, and she began taking on water. The ship had not been adequately repaired during the long layover on Cimbonbon. The leak was worse than ever, and she was in danger in losing her cargo of spices.

With her sister ship in distress, Pigafetta recorded, "*Victoria* returned to its anchorage, and we immediately began to lighten *Trinidad* to see whether we could repair it. We found that the water was rushing in as through a pipe, but we were unable to find where it was coming in. All that and the next day we did nothing but work the pump." The work was exhausting but necessary. Full of spices, the flagship of the fleet was on the verge of sinking at her mooring. The loss of *Trinidad* would be a disaster, depriving the armada of the rewards of its long sought-after spices. Even worse, *Victoria* lacked room to hold the crews of both vessels.

It was just the sort of mishap that Magellan would likely have prevented. *Trinidad* had fallen into disrepair from sheer neglect, and with that ship disabled, the officers' decision to burn *Concepción* returned to haunt them. Not even Magellan would have risked taking only one ship all the way from the Spice Islands back to Spain.

When Almanzor heard about *Trinidad*, "he sent five men into the water to see whether they could discover the hole. They remained more than one half hour under water, but were quite unable to find the leak." After an anxious night, Almanzor reappeared with the men at dawn. But even these men failed to locate the leak, and when they emerged from the water, the king broke down. Who among them, he pleaded, would be able to return to Spain now and tell King Charles about the loyalty of the king of Tidore?

Pigafetta and the others tried to calm the hysterical ruler by describing their new plan for returning to Spain: Elcano would take

Victoria by herself on a westerly course, which was the most direct route back to Spain. But this course brought special dangers because it crossed the Portuguese hemisphere, as defined by the Treaty of Tordesillas. If Portuguese navigators captured a Spanish ship loaded with spices in their waters, they would be ruthless.

Trinidad's course home promised even greater risks. Once she was repaired, she would try to catch favorable winds carrying her along an easterly course toward what is now Panama, where her cargo would be transferred to mules. The beasts would carry the spices to another Spanish fleet heading for Seville. But this plan was based on a deeply flawed conception of the American landmass.

Almanzor pledged no less than 250 carpenters to perform the work required to return *Trinidad* to seaworthiness, and he promised to treat all the sailors who remained behind as if they were his own sons. The king's sincerity and generosity finally wore away the officers' skepticism: "He spoke these words so earnestly that he made us all weep."

Before *Victoria* left Tidore, the crew members loaded her with as many cloves as they could salvage from *Trinidad*, but once they saw *Victoria* riding low in the water, "mistrusting that the ship might open," they lightened the load by removing sixty quintals of cloves and storing the spices in the trading house.

Victoria was so dilapidated that many crew members refused to board her. So the crew divided itself between the two ships, each man seeking the lesser of two evils: *Victoria*, the flimsy vessel that would depart for Spain immediately, or the much larger *Trinidad*, which needed weeks if not months of repairs before she could begin her journey home.

Carvalho was designated captain of *Trinidad*, and Elcano, now the captain general, took over the command of *Victoria*. Pigafetta faced the most critical decision of the entire journey: Which ship would he join? His instinct for survival had stood many tests, and he elected to go along with Elcano aboard *Victoria*. Although he hated the Basque mariner, he clearly had more confidence in Elcano's seamanship than in Carvalho's.

———————

Early on the morning of December 21, Almanzor came aboard *Victoria* for the last time, delivering two pilots, paid for by the crew, to guide the ship safely through the maze of islands and shoals. Finally, at noon, it was time to leave the Spice Islands.

This should have been a festive occasion, the ship bulging with spices, but the damage to *Trinidad* had dramatically altered the final leg of this voyage around the world. Despite the obstacles they had faced, the men of the armada had always taken comfort in the knowledge that they had extra ships at their disposal. Even two ships had a reasonable chance of making it back to Seville, but one ship was hardly up to the task, no matter how skillful the crew's seamanship or how favorable the winds. One ship, alone, was always at the mercy of storms, shoals, pirates, termites, or faulty navigation. On the high seas, no king could protect them, and at least one sovereign, Manuel of Portugal, wanted them dead. Yet the men of the armada had no choice but to face the tests that lay ahead.

CHAPTER FOURTEEN

GHOST SHIP

Victoria headed south, calling at a small island to load firewood, then resumed her course. She was to sail across the Indian Ocean toward one of the most dangerous places for sailors in the world: the Cape of Good Hope, at the southern tip of Africa.

The final leg of the very first journey around the world should have been an occasion for relief among the homeward-bound crew members, but it was not. The character of the expedition had changed completely; the Armada de Molucca finally had its spices, but it had lost its soul. Only survival mattered now.

Even if the crew survived the voyage home, they were anxious about the reception they would receive in Spain. They had no knowledge of *San Antonio*'s arrival in Seville a year earlier, and no inkling that the mutineers aboard that ship had succeeded in discrediting Magellan. For all Elcano and *Victoria*'s crew knew, they would be arrested and jailed for treason the moment they tied up at the dock.

Two days after Christmas, the ship found anchorage, where the crew gathered fresh—and much needed—supplies, along with an Indonesian pilot who knew his way around the islands. Under his guidance, the crew sailed on as if in a trance, heading south, avoiding Moors and cannibals, coral reefs and hidden sandbars, and pirates. As a lone vessel packed with spices, *Victoria* was especially vulnerable to predators.

On January 8, 1522, *Victoria* entered the Banda Sea, extending west of the Moluccas, and the weather suddenly changed. A squall nearly shattered the ship, and when the seas calmed, *Victoria* limped to an anchorage close to shore. The next day, divers inspecting the hull discovered extensive damage, and the men carefully hauled the vessel onto a beach for repairs and caulking.

The inhabitants of this island, known as Malua, shocked even the toughest sailors. They were, said Pigafetta, "savage and bestial, and eat human flesh," and their appearance combined the frightening and the outlandish. "They wear their beards wrapped in leaves and thrust into small bamboo tubes." Pigafetta judged them to be "the ugliest people in the Indies." Despite the inhabitants' bizarre appearance, the sailors offered trinkets, and both sides quickly made peace.

Two weeks later, with repairs to the hull completed, Elcano gave the order to resume the voyage home. At the island of Timor, towering nearly ten thousand feet above the shimmering surface of the Pacific, Elcano ordered a party of sailors to go ashore in search of a bargaining chip: "Inasmuch we had but few things, and hunger was constraining us, we restrained in the ship a chief and his son from another village." With their hostages in hand, the armada's officers proceeded to bargain for the food they so desperately needed. The strategy worked as planned, and the islanders delivered a delicious ransom of six buffalo, a dozen goats, and as many pigs to the grateful yet greedy sailors in exchange for the hostages' freedom.

Once the slaughtered beasts had been loaded, *Victoria* set sail once more, headed for her meeting with destiny at the Cape of Good Hope.

Within days of leaving Timor, struggling against the elements, *Victoria* became the plaything of the unstable weather systems of the southern latitudes. Pigafetta warned, "It is the largest and most dangerous cape in the world." And he was right. The Cape of Good Hope was extremely hazardous and barely navigable even by the most seaworthy of ships and the most experienced of captains.

Juan Sebastián Elcano had never experienced anything like the powerful, confused winds and riptides of the Cape of Good Hope; navigating around it would tax his skills, his patience, and his bravery to the fullest extent. Many of the crew wanted to jump ship at the island of Madagascar rather than risk it, even though doing so would mean a life of exile and slavery, because Madagascar was a Portuguese stronghold.

Meanwhile, fifteen hundred miles east, *Trinidad* prepared to leave the island of Tidore. On April 6, after more than four months of repairs, she finally weighed anchor and unfurled her sail. The ship carried a full load of spices, one thousand quintals of cloves—fifty tons!—more than enough to justify the expense of the entire voyage.

Gonzalo Gómez de Espinosa commanded Magellan's former flagship. As the fleet's master-at-arms, Espinosa was a loyal servant to King Charles, and he had helped Magellan maintain authority over his rebellious crew. But as a captain, Espinosa was hopelessly out of his element. Without Magellan to advise and protect him, it became apparent that the challenge of guiding *Trinidad* halfway around the world to Spain was beyond him.

Leaving behind four men to operate a trading post on the island of Tidore, Espinosa backtracked and sailed along an easterly course through waters the fleet had already explored. But soon after his departure, the monsoon season started, bringing with it seemingly endless storms and drenching rains.

"After ten days of sailing," according to pilot Ginés de Mafra, "they arrived at one of the Islands of the Thieves." Their position was close to the armada's first landfall after her ninety-eight-day ordeal of crossing the Pacific during the voyage out. "There Gonzalo de Vigo stayed, much tired of the travails." He wasn't the only one to desert—in all, three crew members fled, preferring to take their chances on a remote Pacific island rather than remaining aboard Espinosa's ship. (Vigo remained in the Philippines for many years and eventually died there; the other two deserters were soon killed by islanders.)

Braving fierce winds, Espinosa sailed as far north as Japan, into frigid waters. Scurvy returned to torment the men, and ultimately claimed the lives of thirty sailors, leaving only twenty to carry on against the odds. Finally, Espinosa came to his senses. "When I saw the people suffering," he wrote, "the contrary weather, and [realized] that I had been at sea for five months, I turned back to the Moluccas, and by the time we got to the Moluccas, . . . it had been seven months at sea without taking [on] any refreshments."

————

As Espinosa approached his goal of returning to Tidore, he received shocking news. On May 13, five weeks after *Trinidad's* departure, a fleet of seven Portuguese ships, all looking for Magellan and the Armada de Molucca, had arrived at the island. Their leader was António de Brito, with a royal appointment as governor of the Spice Islands.

His Portuguese soldiers, heavily armed, imprisoned the four crew members Espinosa had left behind at the trading post. Then Brito turned his attention to Almanzor, the king of Tidore, demanding to know how he could have allowed the Spanish to erect a trading post on his island. Almanzor pleaded for mercy, explaining that the Spanish had forced him to yield, but now that Captain Brito had come to rescue Almanzor from the Spanish, he would gladly switch his loyalty back. Brito reclaimed the Spice Islands in the name of Portugal.

Espinosa dispatched a boat bearing a letter for Captain Brito, begging for mercy. His ship was in bad condition, down to its last anchor; one storm could send it to the bottom. And he was in desperate need of supplies. Magellan would never have been so foolish as to write a letter to the Portuguese captain who was trying to capture him, and the last thing he would have done was to reveal his whereabouts to the enemy. He would have known there was no chance of mercy from the Portuguese.

The letter only made Brito gloat. A few days later, a Portuguese caravel with twenty armed men stormed the harbor where Espinosa had sought refuge. The soldiers boarded *Trinidad*, expecting to overwhelm the crew, but were repelled by the spectacle of a ship on the verge of sinking; men near death, too weak to move; and a foul and unhealthy stench that no one dared to brave. Everything Espinosa had said in his letter to Brito was true: *Trinidad* and her crew were in desperate condition and offered no threat to the Portuguese.

Unmoved, the Portuguese soldiers arrested Espinosa and ordered the Portuguese sailors to sail Magellan's rotten and decaying flagship to Ternate. There Brito took possession of *Trinidad*'s papers, logbooks, and navigation instruments. Included in the haul were the diary of Andrés de San Martín, the fleet's astronomer, and, it is said, Magellan's personal logbook. Brito ordered the ship stripped of all her sails and rigging, and in this condition she rode helplessly at anchor when a severe storm hit the island. The winds smashed apart the remains of the once-proud ship, her precious cargo of cloves sank, and the splintered remnants of her hull washed up on shore. The flagship of the Armada de Molucca ended up as driftwood.

When Brito examined the logbooks, he became enraged because they contained evidence of the armada's route through Portuguese waters. Even worse, Brito and later chroniclers discovered that the astronomer, Andrés de San Martín, had secretly altered the location of various lands to hide the fact that the ships had wandered into the Portuguese hemisphere, at least as it was defined by the Treaty of Tordesillas. With this information, Brito had his motive for revenge.

His first victim was Pedro Afonso de Lorosa, the Portuguese traitor who had joined the fleet when it first called at the Spice Islands. He was beheaded. Brito spared the lives of a boatswain and a carpenter, forcing them into service for the Portuguese. He sent the rest of the crew to help build a fortress under construction on the island of Ternate. The timber used to construct the fort, and the cannon to protect it, came from the wreck of *Trinidad*.

Now there was only one ship left of the five comprising the original Armada de Molucca. *Victoria*, under Elcano's command, had tried again and again to set a course around the Cape of Good Hope, each time without success but without serious damage, either. The ship battled currents, giant waves, and gales that can change from northeasterly to a southwesterly in a matter of minutes. Winds can reach up to one hundred miles an hour, and *Victoria* experienced blasts powerful enough to damage her fore-topmast and main yard. Sixty-foot-high killer waves, monstrous walls of water, inflicted additional misery.

The constant battering exhausted the crew, and simply finding a quiet moment to consume a few handfuls of barely edible food, usually rice, came to seem like a major accomplishment, and getting through the day a miracle of sorts.

Just when it seemed that the cape was impassable, the wind shifted slightly and the storms briefly stopped. Elcano seized the moment. Fighting churning waters, sailing as close to the wind as he dared, Elcano finally drove his ship around the Cape of Good Hope. It was May 22, 1522, the winds had subsided, and *Victoria* was at last able to proceed on a northerly course.

Although *Victoria* had passed the supreme navigational test, the torments afflicting her crew were not over yet. On June 8, 1522, she crossed the equator for the fourth time since leaving Spain. "Then we sailed northwest for two months continually without taking on any fresh food or water," Pigafetta reported. Inevitably, scurvy returned to devastate the crew. "Twenty-one men died during that short time." The victims included Martín de Magallanes, Magellan's young nephew, who had sailed as a passenger.

On Wednesday, July 9, they reached Santiago, the largest of the Cape Verde Islands, off the coast of West Africa. The islands were a center for Portuguese commerce, and the seas surrounding them were familiar to Portuguese mariners—too familiar, in fact, for *Victoria's* safety. The farther north she journeyed, the more likely she was to encounter Portuguese authorities.

As soon as *Victoria* dropped anchor, Elcano dispatched a longboat for food the starving crew so urgently needed. Fearing that the Portuguese would likely pounce, the men crafted a cover story. Their version left out any mention of their visit to the Spice Islands, the precious cloves they were carrying, Magellan's death, the mutinies, their struggles around the Cape of Good Hope, and, most important of all, their nearly complete circumnavigation of the globe. Instead, they posed as an unlucky, storm-battered Spanish cargo ship hardly worth troubling over. The cover seemed to work, and Pigafetta gloated, "With those good words, and with our merchandise, we got two boatloads of rice."

But as *Victoria* was about to slip away from Santiago, Elcano made a mistake, and it was a serious one. "On Monday, the fourteenth [of July]," wrote Francisco Albo, "we sent the ship's boat ashore for more rice. It returned the next day, and went back for another load. We waited until night, but it did not return. Then we waited until the next day, but it never returned." Something had gone wrong, although no one aboard the ship knew what it was. While on the island, one of the sailors let slip that their captain general, Ferdinand Magellan, was dead, raising the suspicions of the authorities.

"We requested them to send us our men and the ship's boat. They replied that they would bear our request to their officials," Pigafetta recorded. "Fearing lest we also be taken prisoner by certain caravels," he went on, "we hastily departed." It was now July 15, 1522.

———

With barely enough men to handle the ship, Elcano took *Victoria* along a northerly course to her meeting with destiny in Spain. Leaks constantly threatened to overwhelm *Victoria*, and the men, in their exhausted condition, were forced to work the pumps night and day simply to stay afloat.

"On Saturday, September 6, 1522, we entered the bay of Sanlúcar with only eighteen men, the majority of them sick, all that were left of the sixty men who had left the Moluccas. Some died of hunger; some deserted at the island of Timor; and some were put to death for crimes," wrote Pigafetta. His reference to "crimes" has given rise to speculation

158

that Elcano had to endure a mutiny during the final weeks of the voyage, and might have sunk to the same level of cruelty as Magellan.

To complete her journey around the world, *Victoria* and her devastated crew had to make one last passage, from the harbor of Sanlúcar de Barrameda along the Guadalquivir River into Seville. Elcano sent for a small boat to tow the battered craft and its exhausted crew to the teeming city, now abuzz with excitement concerning the extraordinary voyage. Although her hull was in such poor condition and leaking so profusely that the men had to keep pumping all the way just to stay afloat, *Victoria* completed her journey along the river to Seville and tied up at a quay on September 10.

Under the scrutiny of representatives of the king and his financiers, dockworkers unloaded the precious cargo that *Victoria* had traveled around the world to collect. Even with the loss of four ships and 242 men, not to mention the ordinary expenses of the voyage such as salaries and equipment, the amount of cloves in *Victoria*'s hold was sufficient to turn a profit for the expedition's backers. The king's agents were pleased to note that the cloves were of first quality, much better than those purchased from merchants who had acquired them in the traditional manner, from middlemen using land routes.

The day after arriving in Seville, the eighteen survivors, dressed only in their ragged shirts and breeches, did penance. Walking barefoot, holding a candle, still getting accustomed to the unusual feeling of solid, unshakable land beneath his feet, Elcano led the emaciated, exhausted pilgrims through Seville's narrow, winding streets to the shrine of Santa María de la Victoria, where they knelt to pray before the statue of the blessed Virgin and Child. The survivors were traumatized, tentative, and humbled by all they had seen and experienced.

Their prayers concluded, the last of the first crew to circle the globe went their separate ways. They shed the rags they had brought with them from the sea, put on new clothing, and went to their modest homes.

———

DE LOS 265 TRIPULANTES QUE AL MANDO DE FERNANDO
MAGALLANES SALIERON DE ESTE PUERTO DE SANLUCAR DE
BARRAMEDA EL DIA 20 DE SEPTIEMBRE DE 1.519 PARA
DAR, POR PRIMERA VEZ, LA VUELTA AL MUNDO, SOLAMEN-
TE VOLVIERON A ESTE MISMO LUGAR DE PARTIDA, EN 6 DE SEP-
TIEMBRE DE 1.522, LOS 18 NAVEGANTES QUE SE CITAN A CONTINUACION:
JUAN SEBASTIAN ELCANO, DE GUETARIA.
FRANCISCO ALBO, DE AXIO.
MIGUEL DE RODAS, DE RODAS.
JUAN DE ACURIO, DE BERMEO.
MARTIN DE YUDICIBUS, DE SAONA.
HERNANDO DE BUSTAMANTE, DE MERIDA.
HANS, DE AGAN.
DIEGO GALLEGO, DE BAYONA DEL MYOR (GALICIA).
NICOLAS DE NAPOLES, DE NAPOL DE ROMANIA.
MIGUEL SANCHEZ DE RODAS, DE RODAS.
FRANCISCO RODRIGUEZ, DE SEVILLA.
JUAN RODRIGUEZ, DE HUELVA.
ANTONIO HERNANDEZ, DE HUELVA.
JUAN DE ARRATIA, DE BILBAO.
JUAN DE SANTANDER, DE CUETO.
VASCO GOMEZ GALLEGO, DE BAYONA DE GALICIA.
JUAN DE ZUBILETA, DE BARACALDO Y
ANTONIO LOMBARDO (PIGAFETTA), NATURAL DE
BIZANCIO, EN LOMBARDIA.
EL EXCMO. AYUNTAMIENTO DE ESTA CIUDAD Y EL ATENEO
SANLUQUEÑO, UNIDOS AMBOS EN UN MISMO SENTIMIENTO DE
VENERACION HACIA LAS GLORIAS DEL PASADO, CONVINIERON
COLOCAR AQUI ESTOS AZULEJOS COMO MEDIO DE CONMEMORAR
DE UN MODO PUBLICO Y PERMANENTE, LA GESTA REFERIDA,
DIGNA DE NO CAER EN EL OLVIDO DE LOS TIEMPOS.
1.956, MAYO 7.

A tablet in the town of Sanlúcar de Barrameda, Spain, lists the surviving members of
the Armada de Molucca.

In a bustling square in Sanlúcar de Barrameda, there is today a small tile plaque mounted high on the stone facade of an old building. The plaque's worn inscription commemorates the eighteen survivors of the first-ever circumnavigation of the globe:

Juan Sebastián Elcano	Captain
Francisco Albo	Pilot
Miguel de Rodas	Master
Juan de Acurio	Boatswain
Martín de Judicibus	Sailor
Hernando de Bustamante	Barber
Hans of Aachen	Gunner
Diego Gallego	Sailor
Nicholas the Greek, of Naples	Sailor
Miguel Sánchez, of Rodas	Sailor
Francisco Rodríguez	Sailor
Juan Rodríguez	Sailor
Antonio Hernandez	Sailor
Juan de Arratia	Sailor
Juan de Santander	Ordinary seaman
Vasco Gomez Gallego	Ordinary seaman
Juan de Zubileta	Page
Antonio Pigafetta	Passenger

In the entire list, only Elcano, the captain; Albo, the pilot; Bustamante, the barber; and Pigafetta, the chronicler, could be considered notable members of the armada's original roster. The others were ordinary men, many in their twenties or even younger, the overlooked servants of more powerful officers and specialists. No matter their status, they had seen more of the world than anyone else before them; by accident or design, their names belong among history's great explorers.

Juan Sebastián Elcano, who took command of Victoria *after Magellan's death and completed the first circumnavigation of the globe.*

CHAPTER FIFTEEN

— AFTER MAGELLAN —

Reveling in the unexpected success of the Armada de Molucca, King Charles sent for Juan Sebastián Elcano and two men of Elcano's choosing to visit him at his residence at Valladolid to provide a full accounting of their heroic deeds. Elcano selected the pilot, Francisco Albo, and the barber, Hernando de Bustamante, to back up his story. As a sign of royal favor, Elcano's delegation received a lavish payment for formal clothes and traveling expenses to Valladolid; they were expected to make an impressive appearance before their sovereign.

Charles warmly received the three world travelers on October 18, 1522, and congratulated them on having reached the Spice Islands through a water route and claiming them for Spain. Aware of what was expected, Elcano presented His Majesty with samples of the spices brought back from the Moluccas, as well as letters from the island chieftains swearing loyalty to the unknown ruler of the distant land.

All that was very impressive, but it was just for show.

Clouds of suspected disloyalty, even mutiny, hung over the survivors' heads. It was whispered that Magellan had been killed not by warriors on Mactan, but by the members of the fleet. Could Elcano have been among the murderers? And there remained conflicting accounts of the bitter mutiny at Port Saint Julian, some blaming the Spanish officers for the uprising and others holding the Portuguese responsible.

To get to the bottom of these stories, the three men—Elcano, Albo, and Bustamante—faced an inquiry conducted by Valladolid's mayor, acting on orders from King Charles himself. Forced to confront the rumors surrounding Magellan's death, Elcano held the Mactanese islanders completely responsible. By burning their hamlet, Elcano implied, Magellan had antagonized them into taking revenge. His explanation went unchallenged and in the end served as the basis of the official determination of the cause of Magellan's death. Meanwhile, King Charles and his advisers were reminded that the survivors had brought them a fortune in spices, a claim to the Spice Islands themselves, a new water route to the islands, and an unequaled mastery of the ocean—all of it priceless.

———

King Charles offered a quarter of his own proceeds from the voyage to the three survivors who had testified in Valladolid. Elcano's bonus included even more: an annual pension, a knighthood, and a coat of arms suitable for the mariner who had sailed around the world. It portrayed a castle, spices, two Malay kings, and a globe, and it bore the following legend:

> *Primus circumdedisti me*
> Thou first circled me.

Of equal importance, Elcano received a royal pardon for his role in the failed mutiny against Magellan's command. Elcano insisted on having the document published, making his pardon complete. He would now be qualified to lead future expeditions for Castile.

Other survivors of the expedition eventually received similar nods of royal favor. Martín Méndez, *Victoria's* purser; Hernando de Bustamante, the barber; and Miguel de Rodas, the master of *Victoria*, each received individual coats of arms commemorating their accomplishments. Gonzalo Gómez de Espinosa, the *aguacil*, endured even greater trials—two years of hard labor at the hands of the Portuguese in Java, followed by three years of prison in Lisbon. After Espinosa regained his freedom, Charles V made amends by conferring noble status and a coat of arms on this long-suffering voyager, along with restoration of his back pay.

In time, the men who had mutinied against Magellan—an entire ship filled with them—were freed from prison and forgiven for their crimes. Álvaro de Mesquita, who had served as captain of *San Antonio* until the mutiny, had been rotting in jail ever since his return to Seville in 1521. With *Victoria's* survivors supporting his story, the diehard Magellan loyalist was also freed in a general amnesty designed to end lingering controversy about the voyage. Having had enough of Spanish justice, Mesquita fled home to Portugal.

————

By far the most authoritative and well-written chronicle of the first voyage around the world flowed from the pen of Antonio Pigafetta, who had faithfully maintained his diary throughout the entire expedition. Pigafetta immediately started writing his own passionate plea for recognition of Magellan's bravery and loyalty to the king and the Catholic Church. He provided eloquent eyewitness testimony about how Magellan had died and, more important, how he had lived.

Leaving Seville, Pigafetta headed directly for Valladolid, where he presented the twenty-one-year-old monarch with "neither gold nor silver, but things very highly esteemed by such a sovereign. Among other things, I gave him a book, written by my hand, concerning all the matters that had occurred day to day during our voyage."

Pigafetta's diplomatic background served him well, because he then gave his account to sovereigns who were often bitter enemies of one another. Pigafetta's thorough and evenhanded distribution of his account ensured Magellan's leading role in the adventure was known to future generations—and, by association, his own. "I made the voyage and saw with my eyes the things hereafter written," Pigafetta vowed, "that I might win a famous name with posterity." After traveling across Europe, Pigafetta returned home to Venice and immediately caused a stir with the details of his voyage.

Although Pigafetta and a few others celebrated Magellan's extraordinary accomplishments, many considered him a traitor, and court historians everywhere prepared to blacken pages with their accusations of his immoral deeds and treason. King João III of Portugal (the son of Manuel I, the monarch who had spurned Magellan) fumed at the news that one of the ships of the Armada de Molucca had

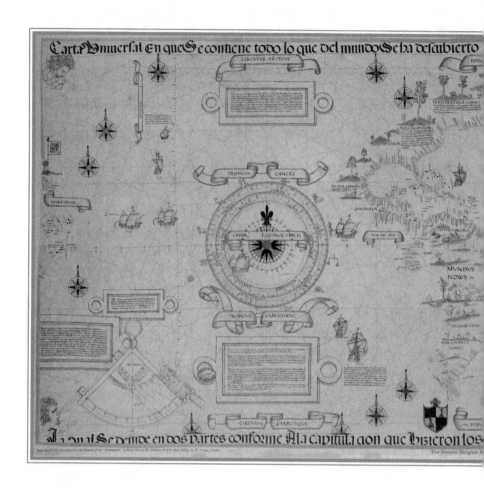

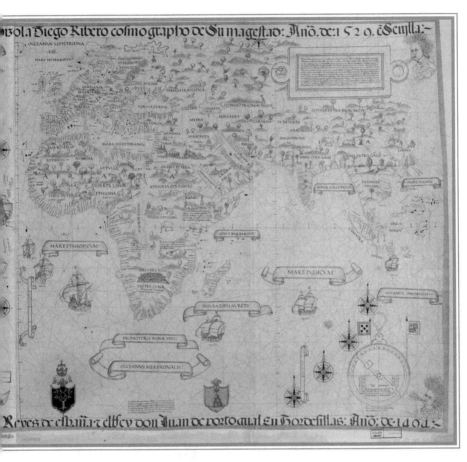

The European view of the world after Magellan's voyage. The Padrón Real, the "official" map of the world produced in 1533 by the Casa de Contratación and carried aboard all Spanish ships, shows the Strait of Magellan and the extent of the Pacific.

returned to Seville with a full load of cloves. He hotly protested to King Charles, insisting that the Spice Islands actually belonged to Portugal. Charles, for his part, patiently but relentlessly pressed for the release of the thirteen men taken prisoner by the Portuguese in the Cape Verde Islands, and they trickled in to Spain in small groups throughout the following year.

———

Victoria's two groups of survivors, for all the hardships they had endured since leaving the Spice Islands, enjoyed a better fate than the sixty-one men who had chosen to sail home aboard *Trinidad.* In 1526, after four miserable years in captivity, Gonzalo Gómez de Espinosa, the former captain, and Ginés de Mafra, the pilot, joined the crew's gunner, Hans Vargue, aboard a ship bound for Lisbon. However, on arrival, the heroic circumnavigators were thrown into jail.

Toughened by years of adversity, Mafra and Espinosa survived their time in a Lisbon prison as they had survived everything else, and upon their release they returned to Seville, only to be jailed again. Their case came to trial in 1527; at last they were found not guilty and released. King Charles granted Espinosa an enormous pension—but the Casa de Contratación, as mean-spirited as ever, withheld it. Outraged, Espinosa sued for twice the amount and, in the end, received only a fraction of the settlement, and even that modest amount was dependent upon his participation in another expedition to the Moluccas. Understandably, Espinosa refused to return to the lands where so many Spaniards had lost their lives and where he had suffered in prison for four long years. He lived out his days in Seville.

———

Spain and Portugal agreed to hold another conference to determine the locations of the Spice Islands and the line of demarcation between Spanish and Portuguese territory. Despite the good intentions of the two nations, the proceedings quickly unraveled. The cosmologists and astronomers continued to argue over longitude and could not even agree on the length of a degree, so the question of where to place the Moluccas remained unresolved. Magellan had crossed the Pacific, it was true, but no one yet knew how to measure the distance he had traveled, except by dead reckoning, a method of estimating distance traveled based on speed and time that was of limited value over long distances. For these reasons, the attempt to redefine the line of demarcation ended in failure. As might be expected, both sides claimed victory—and possession of the Spice Islands.

Blatantly ignoring the conference, King Charles splurged on an extravagant follow-up expedition to the Moluccas, without regard to cost or to the risks involved. In an eerie reenactment of Magellan's voyage, just one of the five original ships of the second Armada de Molucca reached the Spice Islands. And of the 450 men who set sail from Spain aboard these ships, only eight lived to see Spain again, an even greater loss of life than Magellan's crew suffered. One of those who perished on this second voyage was Juan Sebastián Elcano, who died of scurvy on August 4, 1526. His body was committed to the deep amid the rolling blue expanses of the Pacific.

Two more failed armadas followed. With each failure, the dream of establishing a Spanish outpost in the Spice Islands and bringing the wealth of the Indies into Spain faded, and the scope of Magellan's accomplishment and determination came to seem greater and greater. Just seven years after Magellan's voyage, King Charles, facing bankruptcy, gave up and returned the islands to the Portuguese.

Not until 1580, fifty-eight years after *Victoria* returned to Seville, did another explorer, English captain Francis Drake, complete a circumnavigation. His voyage took him through the Strait of Magellan. To accomplish the feat, Drake relied on the knowledge so painfully and heroically discovered by Magellan.

———

Little *Victoria*, the first ship to complete a circumnavigation, was repaired, sold to a merchant, and returned to service, a workhorse of the Spanish conquest of the Americas. As late as 1570, she was still crossing the Atlantic. En route to Seville from the Antilles, she disappeared without a trace; all hands on board were lost. It is assumed that she encountered a mid-Atlantic storm that sent her to the bottom, her wordless epitaph written on the restless waves.

In 1531, one of the first accurate maps of the Strait of Magellan appeared. In time, the name *Magellan* came to designate only the strait—no lands and in fact none of the territories that the captain general once dreamed of leaving to his heirs. At least, such was the case on earth. In the heavens, his name came to be associated with the two dwarf galaxies he had discovered, the Magellanic Clouds, visible in the Southern Hemisphere.

Although no continent or country was named after Magellan, he and the Armada de Molucca confronted the intellectual and spiritual limitations of their time with the ultimate reality check—traveling around the globe. They had made records for others to study, expanding Europeans' knowledge of the world. Although they had circled the globe, the world was now a larger place than previously imagined, not smaller. Seven thousand miles had been added to the globe's circumference, as well as a massive body of water, the Pacific Ocean.

They had learned that, beyond Europe, people existed in astonishing numbers and variety, as tall as the giants of Patagonia and as short as the warriors of the Philippines, as generous as the courtiers of Borneo and as violent as the inhabitants of Mactan. Banished were phenomena such as boiling water at the equator and a magnetic island capable of pulling the nails from passing ships. All these discoveries came at the cost of over two hundred lives and extreme hardship. No previous expedition had been as drawn-out and complicated as this one; no later expedition during the Age of the Discovery would equal it for ambition and bravery. It was, and remains, the most important and adventurous ocean voyage in history.

The Ambassador's Globe, produced in about 1526. A line shows Magellan's path across the Pacific—the earliest known cartographic depiction of his voyage.

ACKNOWLEDGMENTS

I am happy to present this new adaptation of *Over the Edge of the World* to younger readers or to those in search of a speedier circumnavigation. And I wish to express my appreciation to Simon Boughton, my intrepid publisher, and his assistants, Zoey Peresman and Claire Dorsett, for their expertise and enthusiasm.

I also wish to thank Sara Fray, my daughter, for her editorial contributions to this version. She also served as a touchstone throughout the adaptation process.

Suzanne Gluck of William Morris Endeavor, my literary agent, provided invaluable assistance with the development of this book every step of the way; it is a privilege to have the benefit of her keen insights and good judgment. Thanks also to the diligent Eve Atterman at WME. At William Morrow, I owe a vast debt of gratitude to the editor of *Over the Edge of the World*, Henry Ferris, for his steadfast belief in this book and for his editorial expertise. I am also grateful to Trish Grader for her enthusiasm and guidance, and I wish to extend additional thanks to Juliette Shapland and Sarah Durand.

Magellan's circumnavigation concerns many different fields, and I conducted research in a wide variety of institutions. In New York, I was fortunate to be able to use the resources of the following institutions: Butler Library, Columbia University; the New York Society Library, where I wish to thank Mark Piel and Susan O'Brien for their help; the Hispanic Society of America; the New York Academy of Medicine Library; and the New York Public Library. I also want to express my appreciation to Columbia University's John Jay Colloquium, led by Peter Pouncey, where, with numerous distinguished colleagues, I had the opportunity to study classical approaches to writing history.

I owe special thanks to the John Carter Brown Library at Brown University, where Richard Ring, reference librarian; Susan Danforth; and Norman Fiering, director, offered support and encouragement. I also received assistance at the Harvard University Archives from Melanie M. Halloran, reference assistant, and Harley P. Holden, university archivist, in researching the papers of the naval historian Samuel Eliot Morison. My appreciation goes to Mrs. Emily Beck Morison for granting me access to the papers. I must also mention the Beinecke Rare Book and Manuscript Library, Yale University, the repository of the Antonio Pigafetta manuscript; the Library of Congress, Manuscript Division, Washington, D.C.; and the Special Collections Department, Brandeis University Libraries, where Susan C. Pyzynski, Eliot Wilczek, and Lisa Long guided me through their documents pertaining to lawsuits arising from Magellan's voyage; the Peabody Library, Johns Hopkins University; and John Hattendorf of the Naval War College in Newport, Rhode Island.

My thanks go also to the NASA scientists who provided up-to-date satellite images of Magellan's route and a better understanding of the physical nature of the globe: James Garvin, NASA's lead scientist for Mars exploration; and Claire Parkinson, project scientist for the Aqua mission. Credit must also go to Marshall Shepherd, research meteorologist, and Chester Koblinsky, head of the Oceans and Ice Branch, for their assistance.

Many other individuals generously offered guidance. In New York, I wish to thank my son, Nick, for his sailing expertise; Wilma and Esteban Cordero; Ed Darrach of Bristed-Manning for travel-related services; Darrell Fennell; Sloan Harris; Emily Nurkin; Roberta Oster; Meredith Palmer; Natalia Tapies; Susan Sparrow; and Susan Shapiro. Thanks also to Jennifer O'Keeffe for research assistance in New York. Others who helped include Daniel Dolgin, good friend and careful reader; Alexandra Roosevelt; Martha Saxton; and Robert Schiffman, MD.

Because primary sources about Magellan exist in several languages, I am indebted to translators including Isabel Cuadrado, Laura Kopp, and Rosa Moran.

In the course of my research trips to Spain, I received assistance from Kristina Cordero, Javier Guardiola, and Víctor Úbeda. In Madrid, I conducted research at the Museo Naval and the Biblioteca Nacional, and in Seville, I consulted the Archive of the Indies, where I am grateful for the assistance of Pilar Lazaro, chief of the Reference Division. Thanks to Francisco Contente Domingues in Portugal, and in Brazil, Alessandra Blocker, my editor at Objetiva.

A highlight of my research for this book was a voyage to South America in January 2001 to travel along Magellan's route through the strait that bears his name. In Patagonia, I wish to thank the captain and crew of M/V *Terra Australis*, on which I sailed, and Jon V. Diamond, my traveling companion.

Notes on Sources

Ferdinand Magellan remains controversial even today; various chroniclers have considered him a tyrant, a traitor, a visionary, and a hero. As befits an explorer who led a multinational crew on a voyage around the world, accounts of his life and circumnavigation have been heavily influenced by divergent manuscript traditions arising from a rich store of primary and important secondary sources in Spanish, French, Portuguese, Latin, and Italian. In recreating Magellan's epic voyage, I generally relied on diverse primary sources—diaries, journals, contemporaneous accounts, royal warrants, and legal testimony. Some important early Magellan sources were translated into English for the first time for use in my book for adult readers, *Over the Edge of the World*. These include a lengthy memoir by Ginés de Mafra, who was one of the survivors; early histories by João de Barros, Antonio de Herrera y Tordesillas, and Gonzalo Fernández de Oviedo y Valdez; and legal documents pertaining to the voyage now archived at Brandeis University in Massachusetts.

The most important (though not the only) source of primary information about the voyages of Magellan and other explorers is the Archive of the Indies in Seville. Martín Fernández de Navarette edited a five-volume compilation of the archive's chief holdings, published in Spanish in 1837, which advanced understanding of Magellan and his era; most of the archive's records pertaining to Magellan's voyage are in volume 4 of that compilation.

As a result of this wealth of primary sources, Spanish historians have relied on earlier works in Spanish, while Portuguese historians have emphasized Portuguese sources and attitudes, often sharply critical of Magellan. More recently, English-language historians have generally portrayed Magellan in a heroic light. In particular, the naval historian Samuel Eliot Morison wrote several chapters on Magellan in his classic work *The European Discovery of America: The Southern Voyages* (1974), to which I acknowledge my debt. F. H. H. Guillemard's *Life of Ferdinand Magellan* (1890) remains useful; since then, new sources and approaches to the era have emerged, making it possible to give a more three-dimensional account of the voyage. Also worthwhile is Tim Joyner's *Magellan* (1992). Martin Torodash's "Magellan Historiography," published in *The Hispanic American Historical Review* 51, no. 2 (May 1971), surveys the entire field.

The best eyewitness account of Magellan's circumnavigation was written by Antonio Pigafetta. His chronicle, written in French, remains one of the most significant documents of the Age of Discovery. In 1969, R. A. Skelton's translation managed to convey a sense of Pigafetta's voice and sensibility; it includes a facsimile of the Pigafetta manuscript in the Beinecke Rare Book and Manuscript Library at Yale University. Pigafetta was not a disinterested source. He was, touchingly, a Magellan loyalist, and as a result, he made only the briefest mention of the various mutinies during the voyage and Magellan's drastic efforts to quell them. In addition, Francisco Albo's pilot's record gives a day-by-day record of the voyage.

Chapter One: The Quest

Concerning the Treaty of Tordesillas, Samuel Eliot Morison's *The European Discovery of America: The Southern Voyages* and Tim Joyner's *Magellan* both contain valuable analyses of the treaty as it affected Magellan's proposed expedition, as does Jean Denucé's *Magellan* (pp. 46–47).

Pedro de Medina's *A Navigator's Universe*, translated by Ursula Lamb, sheds light on the subject of Renaissance cosmology, as does Alison Sandman's accomplished PhD dissertation, *Cosmographers vs. Pilots*.

For more on spices and the spice trade throughout history, see notes to chapter 13. J. H. Parry's *The Discovery of the Sea* summarizes Portuguese ocean exploration.

For extended discussions of Magellan's ancestry, see Joyner (p. 309); Morison, *The European Discovery of America: The Southern Voyages* (pp. 327–29); and Manuel Villas-Boas, *Os Magalhães*.

Among the many accounts of Magellan's early career are F. H. H.

Guillemard, *The Life of Ferdinand Magellan*; Charles McKew, *So Noble a Captain*; and Samuel Eliot Morison, *The European Discovery of America: The Southern Voyages*. Joyner (pp. 33–57) is especially robust.

Leonard Y. Andaya's *The World of Maluku* mentions the extreme sensitivity of Portuguese maps (p. 9). Magellan's dealings with the Barbosa clan are described by Morison, *The European Discovery of America: The Southern Voyages* (p. 333), and Denucé (p. 168). Roger Craig Smith's PhD dissertation, *Vanguard of Empire*, offers background about the Casa de Contratación (pp. 32–33).

Donald D. Brand's articles in *The Pacific Basin* and Mairin Mitchel's *Elcano* (p. 69) discuss Serrão, whose correspondence with Magellan was lost in the Lisbon earthquake of 1755; all that survives are accounts of it in the records of early Portuguese historians.

Martín Fernández de Navarette, *Colección de los viajes y descubrimientos que hicieron por mar los españoles desde fines del siglo XV*, vol. 4 (pp. 121–22), contains the document formally authorizing Magellan. An English translation can be found in Emma Helen Blair and James Alexander Robertson's *The Philippine Islands: 1493–1898*, vol. 1 (pp. 271–75).

Chapter Two: The Man without a Country

Magellan's distraught letter to King Charles can be found in Virginia Benitz Licuanan and José Llavador Mira, eds., *The Philippines Under Spain* (pp. 11–13). The original mentions placing four flags on the capstan, but it is unlikely that piece of machinery would be used for that purpose; a mast is far more likely. For more, see Samuel Eliot Morison, *The European Discovery of America: The Southern Voyages* (pp. 340–41).

King Charles's correspondence about Magellan's voyage is reproduced in Emma Helen Blair and James Alexander Robertson, *The Philippine Islands: 1493–1898*, vol. 1 (pp. 277–79 and 280–92). For Magellan's sailing orders, see Martín Fernández de Navarrete, *Colección de los viajes y descubrimientos que hicieron por mar los españoles desde fines del siglo XV*, vol. 4. (pp. 130–52) and Blair and Robertson (pp. 256–59).

Documents pertaining to Ruy Faleiro's role in the expedition are reproduced in Navarrete, vol. 4 (p. 497), and in Ignacio Fernández Vial and Guadalupe Fernández Morente, *La primera vuelta al mundo* (pp. 44–45).

The list of navigational supplies carried by the fleet comes from Vial and Morente (pp. 85–86).

Documents concerning Fonseca's dealings with Aranda are contained in Navarette, vol. 2. Although it lacks source notes, Charles McKew Parr's biography, *So Noble a Captain* (p. 230), is strong on preparations for the voyage, including Fonseca's machinations.

Vial and Morente discuss the Seville waterfront (pp. 95–96) and the armada's provisions (p. 128).

The Casa de Contratación's efforts to rein in Magellan are detailed in Vial and Morente (p. 51) and documented in Navarrete, vol. 5. Jean Denucé's *Magellan* discusses Magellan's packing the roster with his relatives (pp. 236–39) and the solemn mass at Santa María de la Victoria (pp. 241–46).

Tim Joyner's *Magellan* (pp. 286–87) has the complete text of Magellan's will, and Denucé (p. 255) tells of Sabrosa's decline after Magellan fled Portugal.

Chapter Three: Neverlands

The prayerful commands are recorded in Pablo Pérez-Malláina, *Spain's Men of the Sea*, tr. Carla Rahn Phillips (p. 69).

The literature of early cartography is vast. A good place for general readers to start is Lloyd A. Brown's *The Story of Maps*, along with Rodney Shirley's *The Mapping of the World*. John Noble Wilford's *Mapmakers* is another valuable summation.

Chapter Four: "The Church of the Lawless"

Details of the contretemps concerning the proper form of address to Magellan come from Samuel Eliot Morison, *The European Discovery of America: The Southern Voyages* (p. 358).

Albo's account of the fleet's arrival in Rio de Janeiro can be found in Henry E. J. Stanley [Lord Stanley of Alderley], ed., *The First Voyage*

Round the World, by Magellan (p. 212). Morison, in *The European Discovery of America: The Southern Voyages* (p. 299), discusses early Portuguese efforts to exploit the region's natural resources. Tim Joyner, in *Magellan* (p. 125), offers details of Carvalho's past.

Details of the sailor's life aboard ships are drawn from Pablo E. Pérez-Malláina, *Spain's Men of the Sea*, tr. Carla Rahn Phillips (pp. 135–59), and Morison, *The European Discovery of America: The Southern Voyages* (pp. 165–71).

Early conceptions of the strait are discussed in F. H. H. Guillemard, *The Life of Ferdinand Magellan* (pp. 191–93), which quotes António Galvão about the "Dragon's taile"; in Justin Winsor, *Narrative and Critical History of America* (p. 107); and in Morison, *The European Discovery of America: The Southern Voyages* (pp. 301–2). See also Mateo Martinic Beros, *Historia del Estrecho de Magallanes*.

Chapter Five: The Crucible of Leadership

Morison, *The European Discovery of America: The Southern Voyages* (p. 365), provides details of Magellan's reconnaissance during the waning days of February. F. H. H. Guillemard, normally scrupulous, mentions in *The Life of Ferdinand Magellan* only one island discovered on February 27, but as Pigafetta makes clear, there were two. See Antonio Pigafetta, *Magellan's Voyage*, tr. R. A. Skelton (p. 46).

What actual animals Magellan and his crew saw in this part of the world is open to debate because Pigafetta did not provide enough details for exact identification. Guillemard and his followers labeled the sea wolves that Magellan's men saw as "fur seals" of the family Otariidae, but that is probably not correct. In general, fur seals do not live in this part of the world, but are found in Australia or more northerly waters, around the Bering Strait, for example. It is more likely that Pigafetta was describing either the sea lion or the elephant seal, both of which are far more common in these latitudes.

The case for Magellan's deliberately obscuring the location of Port Saint Julian is made by Jean Denucé, *Magellan*, whose Portuguese sources might have imputed sinister motives to Magellan and his pilots where none existed. Nevertheless, there are a number of strong hints that as the voyage proceeded Magellan came to realize he had sailed into Portuguese waters, and it was too late for him to do anything about it except hope he was not caught.

Eyewitness accounts of the mutiny in Port Saint Julian can be found in Martín Fernández de Navarette, *Colección de los viajes y descubrimientos que hicieron por mar los españoles desde fines del siglo XV*; Elcano's comment can be found on p. 288. See also Tim Joyner, *Magellan* (pp. 284 and 291).

Chapter Six: Castaways

Samuel Eliot Morison, in *The European Discovery of America: The Southern Voyages* (p. 372), quotes praise for Magellan's industriousness. An account of *Santiago's* ill-fated reconnaissance mission appears in Henry E. J. Stanley [Lord Stanley of Alderley], ed., *The First Voyage Round the World, by Magellan* (p. 250).

Pigafetta's sketchy description of the *Santiago* crew's efforts to survive the trek back to Port Saint Julian is ably supplemented by F. H. H. Guillemard, *The Life of Ferdinand Magellan*, and especially by Antonio de Herrera y Tordesillas, *The General History of the Vast Continent and Islands of America* (pp. 17–18).

Concerning the first signs of Indians in Port Saint Julian, Pigafetta describes the unexpected appearance of a "giant" on the beach, but de Mafra more plausibly recalls the appearance of smoke prior to the giant's arrival. Pigafetta's account of these Indians appears in *Magellan's Voyage*, tr. R. A. Skelton (pp. 47–50), Guillemard (p. 183), and Herrera y Tordesillas (p. 19).

Tim Joyner, in *Magellan* (p. 150), describes the plight of Cartagena and Pero Sánchez de la Reina, as does Morison, in *The European Discovery of America: The Southern Voyages* (p. 375).

Chapter Seven: Dragon's Tail

For early misconceptions of the strait, see J. H. Parry, *The Discovery of the Sea* (p. 248) and Samuel Eliot Morison, *The European Discovery of America: The Southern Voyages* (pp. 382–83).

Although Magellan staked the success of the expedition on navigating the strait, he reluctantly revealed that he had an alternate plan. "Had we not discovered the Strait," Pigafetta informs us, "the Captain General had determined to go as far as seventy-five degrees toward the Atlantic Pole. There in that latitude, during the summer season, there is no night, or if there is any night it is but short, and so in the winter with the day."

Other descriptions of the strait are drawn from Morison, *The European Discovery of America: The Southern Voyages* (pp. 390–91); Charles Darwin, *Voyage of the Beagle* (pp. 196–97, 203); and Antonio de Herrera y Tordesillas (chapter 14). Charles McKew Parr, in *So Noble a Captain*, relates a dramatic encounter between "a half dozen naked Indians" paddling a canoe and Magellan's fleet. But none of the diarists mention it (Pigafetta, fascinated by indigenous tribes, surely would have), nor do other historians. In the absence of sources, this incident lacks a basis in fact.

Magellan's desire to persist in the voyage is related by Denucé, p. 288, and by Herrera y Tordesillas (chapter 15). Tim Joyner, in *Magellan* (p. 276), discusses Estêvão Gomes's resentment. Herrera y Tordesillas says the mutineers killed Mesquita, but as numerous other accounts demonstrate, that was not the case.

Magellan's and San Martín's important letters appear in João de Barros's *Da Asia*, translated for this book by Víctor Úbeda. See also Henry E. J. Stanley [Lord Stanley of Alderley], *The First Voyage Round the World, by Magellan* (pp. 177–78). Barros retrieved the documents from the papers of San Martín, later seized by the Portuguese. In Barros's words, "We do not deem it unfitting to include here the contents of such orders, as well as San Martín's reply, so that it can be seen, not by our words, but by their own, the condition in which they found themselves, and also Magellan's purpose with regard to the route that he planned to follow in case the way he wished to find should fail him."

Pigafetta and Albo disagree on the precise date the armada sailed from the western mouth of the strait. Pigafetta gives the date

as November 28, and Albo as November 26. The discrepancy could
be explained in various ways; for example, Pigafetta and Albo could
have selected different landmarks to mark the strait's end. See Morison,
The European Discovery of America: The Southern Voyages
(pp. 400–401).

Chapter Eight: A Race against Death

Regarding the Southern Cross: The earth wobbles slightly on its axis,
and this movement leads to an apparent change in the position of
the stars over a long period of time. The phenomenon is known as
precession: the stars precess one another in declination, their relative
position in the sky. Over time, precession has brought the cross south,
and it can now be seen only at latitudes south of 25 degrees.

Magellan's failure to make a landfall in the Pacific before Guam
has long prompted questions. One school of thought holds that he was
actually farther north than his chroniclers indicated, and distant from
all islands. Although all the eyewitnesses—Albo, Pigafetta, and
Mafra—agree that the armada headed west into the Pacific at the
approximate latitude of Valparaiso, Chile, others have suggested
that the diarists falsified their accounts to conceal the true location
of the Spice Islands, in case they were found to be in the Portuguese
part of the world rather than the Spanish. The assumption makes little
sense because they wrote their accounts for different purposes: Pigafetta
wrote to glorify Magellan and ingratiate himself with European nobility;
Albo wrote to keep track of their whereabouts; and Mafra dictated his
account years later, when the location of the Spice Islands was no
longer controversial.

Chapter Nine: A Vanished Empire

Much of the information in this chapter is drawn directly from Pigafetta's
account, which eloquently describes the armada's Pacific passage.

For an extended and valuable discussion of Magellan's first landfall
in the Pacific, see Robert F. Rogers and Dirk Anthony Ballendorf,

"Magellan's Landfall in the Mariana Islands." The authors re-created the landfall to be precise about the fleet's movements; however, alterations wrought by erosion can compromise the value of such exercises. Also worth consulting is Robert F. Rogers's book, *Destiny's Landfall*, for details of Chamorran culture.

For a fascinating account of island navigation systems in theory and practice, see Ben Finney, *Voyage of Rediscovery* (especially pp. 56–64).

Louise Levathes's *When China Ruled the Seas* is a reliable guide to the subject written in English. Gavin Menzies's *1421* suggests that the Treasure Fleet reached the Caribbean and perhaps completed a circumnavigation a hundred years before Magellan. However, hard evidence to prove these tantalizing assertions is sorely lacking.

As his candidate for the first person to complete a circumnavigation, Samuel Eliot Morison, in *The European Discovery of America: The Southern Voyages* (p. 435), nominates Magellan's slave Enrique. Morison argues that Magellan's voyage brought Enrique back to his point of origin.

For a discussion of the armada's weaponry, see Charles Boutell, *Arms and Armour in Antiquity and the Middle Ages* (p. 243), and Charles McKew Parr, *So Noble a Captain* (p. 383). Roger Craig Smith's PhD dissertation, *Vanguard of Empire*, offers more specialized information on the subject. Also recommended are Courtlandt Canby, *A History of Weaponry*; John Hewitt, *Ancient Armour and Weapons in Europe*; and Kenneth Macksey, *The Penguin Encyclopedia of Weapons and Military Technology*.

Chapter Ten: The Final Battle

Two very different facets of Pigafetta's wide-ranging interests are on display in his account of Magellan's visit to Cebu. As a former papal diplomat, Pigafetta was duty-bound, but also genuinely moved, by the captain general's efforts to convert Filipinos.

Simon Winchester describes a reenactment of the battle between

Magellan and Lapu Lapu in "After Dire Straits, An Agonizing Haul Across the Pacific" (pp. 84–95).

Chapter Eleven: Ship of Mutineers

Details concerning Enrique's actions are drawn not only from the accounts by Pigafetta and others mentioned in the text but also from Gonzalo Fernández de Oviedo y Valdez's *Historia general y natural de las Indias* (pp. 13ff.). Jean Denucé, in *Magellan* (pp. 323–26), adds to the picture of the massacre's aftermath. See also Samuel Eliot Morison, *The European Discovery of America: The Southern Voyages* (pp. 438–41), and Martín Fernández de Navarette, *Colección de los viajes y descubrimientos que hicieron por mar los españoles desde fines del siglo XV.*

Concerning *San Antonio*'s return to Spain, F. H. H. Guillemard, in *The Life of Ferdinand Magellan* (p. 215), remarks that Argensola, an early and occasionally inaccurate historian, states that Cartagena and the priest were rescued by *San Antonio*, but no records support this claim. Although Guillemard (p. 216) believes *San Antonio* ran low on food during the return journey, that was likely not the case, for she carried the entire fleet's provisions. It is possible that those aboard *San Antonio* invented this story to gain sympathy.

The official reports and orders concerning the mutiny of *San Antonio* and her paltry contents can be found in Virginia Benitz Licuanan and José Llavador Mira, eds., *The Philippines Under Spain* (pp. 17, 24–28, and 43–44). See also Denucé (p. 293). Tim Joyner, in *Magellan* (p. 159), says that Mesquita had to pay for his trial-related costs.

Chapter Twelve: Survivors

Juan Sebastián Elcano's ascent and the problems facing the Armada de Molucca after Magellan's death are set forth in Mairin Mitchell's *Elcano* (see especially pp. 42–48 and 63–64).

Samuel Eliot Morison, in *The European Discovery of America: The Southern Voyages* (p. 442), describes Palawan. Albo's exasperation while trying to reach Brunei can be found in Henry E. J. Stanley [Lord Stanley of Alderley], ed., *The First Voyage* (pp. 226–27).

Chapter Thirteen: Arrival in Paradise

On the subject of Francisco Serrão's curious odyssey in the Spice Islands, F. H. H. Guillemard, in *The Life of Ferdinand Magellan*, offers several unsubstantiated theories. According to one scenario, he was "poisoned by a Malay woman who acted under Portuguese orders." But Guillemard also cites Argensola's assertion that Serrão was not poisoned at all; rather, he was sent back to India, and he died aboard ship (p. 281).

Anyone wanting to learn more about cloves should start by consulting Frederic Rosengarten Jr.'s *Book of Spices* (especially pp. 200–204). Much of the information about spices in this chapter is drawn from this comprehensive and entertaining reference work. Other useful works on the subject include John Parry's *The Story of Spices* (1953) and Bruno Laurioux's article "Spices in the Medieval Diet." Also of interest is M. N. Pearson, ed., *Spices in the Indian Ocean World*.

Chapter Fourteen: Ghost Ship

Espinosa's sad comment about turning back to the Moluccas is in Rodrigue Lévesque, ed., *History of Micronesia* (p. 306).

Much of what is known about *Trinidad's* tragic end comes from João de Barros's *Da Asia*, an account skewed in favor of the Portuguese. Barros (chapter 10) states that António de Brito discovered the armada's attempts to alter the locations of various lands, and F. H. H. Guillemard, in *The Life of Ferdinand Magellan* (p. 303), approvingly quotes Brito's callous report to the Portuguese crown about the armada's survivors. Barros twisted events so that Brito emerges as the savior of Magellan's men, when in fact he was happy to let them die.

Chapter Fifteen: After Magellan

Mairin Mitchell, in *Elcano* (pp. 178–82), provides the relevant documents pertaining to the subsequent inquiry into the expedition. Gonzalo Gómez de Espinosa's last days are accounted for by Tim Joyner, in *Magellan* (pp. 265, 277–78), and Samuel Eliot Morison, in *The European Discovery of America: The Southern Voyages* (p. 456).

Accounts of Juan Sebastián Elcano's last voyage and death can be found in Mitchell (pp. 148–57); Morison (pp. 475–83); J. H. Parry, *The Discovery of the Sea* (p. 257); and Charles E. Nowell, ed., *Magellan's Voyage Around the World* (p. 338).

Lawrence C. Wroth's article "The Early Cartography of the Pacific" (pp. 149–50) details the struggle between Spain and Portugal for the Spice Islands.

The tale of *Victoria's* final voyage is told by J. H. Parry, in *The Discovery of the Sea* (p. 261); Joyner (p. 243); and Mitchell (pp. 106–7).

BIBLIOGRAPHY

Books

Alcocer Martínez, Mariano. *Don Juan Rodríguez Fonseca: Estudia Crítica Biográfica.* Valladolid: Imprenta de la Casa Católica, 1923.

Andaya, Leonard Y. *The World of Maluku.* Honolulu: University of Hawaii Press, 1993.

Andrews, William. *Bygone Punishments.* London: William Andrews & Co., 1899.

Arber, Edward. *The First Three English Books on America.* New York: Kraus Reprint, 1971.

Baker, J. *The History of the Inquisition.* Westminster: O. Payne, 1736.

Baker, J. N. L. *A History of Geographical Discovery and Exploration.* Boston: Houghton Mifflin, 1931.

Barbosa, Duarte. *The Book of Duarte Barbosa,* tr. Mansel Longworth Dames. New Delhi: Asian Educational Society, 1989. (Originally published in 1812.)

———. *A Description of the Coasts of East Africa and Malabar,* tr. Henry E. J. Stanley. London: Hakluyt Society, 1866.

Barros Arana, Diego. *Vida i viajes de Hernando de Magallanes.* Santiago de Chile: Imprenta Nacional, 1864.

Barros, João de. *Da Asia: Decada Terceira.* Lisboa: Na Régia Officina Typografica: 1777.

Bates, Robert L., and Julia A. Jackson, eds. *Dictionary of Geological Terms.* New York: Anchor Books, 1984.

Blair, Emma Helen, and James Alexander Robertson, eds. *The Philippine Islands: 1493–1898,* vol. 1. Mandalyong, Rizal: Cachos Hermanos, 1973.

Benson, E. F. *Magellan.* London: John Lane, 1929.

Birmingham, Stephen. *The Grandees: America's Sephardic Elite.* New York: Harper & Row, 1971.

Blázquez, Antonio, and Delgado Aguilera, eds. *Descripción de los reinos, costas, puertos e islas que hay desde el Cabo de Buena Esperanza hasta* los *Leyquios, por Fernando de Magallanes; Libro que trata del descubrimiento y principio del Estrecho que se llama de Magallanes, por Ginés de Mafra; y Descripción de parte del Japón*. Madrid: Publicaciones de la Real Sociedad Geográfica, 1920.

Boorstin, Daniel J. *The Discoverers*. New York: Random House, 1983.

Bourne, Edward Gaylord. *Discovery, Conquest, and Early History of the Philippine Islands*. Cleveland: Arthur H. Clark, 1907.

———. *Spain in America: 1450–1580*. New York: Harper & Brothers, 1904.

Boutell, Charles. *Arms and Armour in Antiquity and the Middle Ages*. New York: D. Appleton & Co., 1870.

———. *The Mediterranean and the Mediterranean World in the Age of Philip II*. 2 vols. New York: Harper & Row, 1972–73.

Brand, Donald D. "Geographical Exploration by the Spaniards" and "Geographical Exploration by the Portuguese." In *The Pacific Basin: A History of Its Geographical Exploration*, ed. Herman R. Friis. New York: American Geographical Society, 1967.

Brown, Lloyd A. *The Story of Maps*. New York: Dover, 1977. (Originally published in 1949.)

Buehr, Walter. *Firearms*. New York: Thomas Y. Crowell, 1967.

Bueno, José María. *Soldados de España: el uniforme militar español desde los Reyes Católicos hasta Juan Carlos I*. Málaga: 1978.

Cabrero Fernandez, Leoncio, ed. *Historia general de Filipinas*. Madrid: Ediciones de Cultura Hispánica, 2000.

Camões, Luiz de. *The Lusíads*, tr. Landeg White. Oxford: Oxford University Press, 1997.

Campbell, John. *The Spanish Empire in America*. London: M. Cooper, 1747.

Canby, Courtlandt. *A History of Weaponry*, vol. 4. New York: Hawthorn Books, 1963.

Carpenter, Kenneth, J. *The History of Scurvy and Vitamin C*. Cambridge: Cambridge University Press, 1986.

Cipolla, Carlo M. *Guns and Sails in the Early Phase of European Expansion, 1400–1700*. London: Collins, 1965.

Colección General de Documentos Relativos a las Islas Filipinas Existentes en el Archivo de Indias de Sevilla. 5 vols. Barcelona: L. Tasso, 1918–23.

Corn, Charles. *The Scents of Eden*. New York: Kodansha International, 1998.

Crane, Nicholas. *Mercator: The Man Who Mapped the Planet*. London: Weidenfeld & Nicholson, 2002.

Crow, John A. *Spain: The Root and the Flower*. New York: Harper & Row, 1975.

Dalrymple, Alexander. *An Historical Collection of the Several Voyages and Discoveries in the South Pacific Ocean*, vol. 1. London: J. Nourse, 1770.

Darwin, Charles. *Voyage of the Beagle*. London: Penguin Books, 1989. (Originally published 1839.)

Denucé, Jean. *Magellan: La Question des Moluques et la Première Circumnavigation du Globe*. In *Mémoires, Académie Royale de Belgique*, vol. 4. Bruxelles: Hayez, 1908–11.

DeVries, Kelly. *Medieval Military Technology*. Lewiston, NY: Broadview Press, 1992.

Diamond, Jared. *Guns, Germs, and Steel: The Fates of Human Societies*. New York: W. W. Norton, 1997.

Diffie, Bailey W., and George D. Winius. *Foundations of the Portuguese Empire, 1415–1580*. Minneapolis: University of Minnesota Press, 1977.

Eliot, Charles William, ed. *Voyages and Travels: Ancient and Modern*. New York: P. F. Collier and Son, 1910.

Faria y Sousa, Manuel de. *The Portugues [sic] Asia*, tr. John Stevens. Westmead, England: Gregg International Publishing, 1971. (Originally published in 1695.)

Finney, Ben. *Voyage of Rediscovery*. Berkeley: University of California Press, 1994.

Frimmer, Steven. *Neverland*. New York: Viking Press, 1976.

Galvão, António [Galvano, Antonio]. *The Discoveries of the World*, tr. Richard Hakluyt. London: Hakluyt Society, 1862. (Originally published in 1601.)

————. *A Treatise on the Moluccas*, tr. Hubert Jacobs. Rome: Jesuit Historical Institute, 1971. (Originally written c. 1544.)

Gerber, Jane S. *The Jews of Spain: A History of the Sephardic Experience*. New York: Free Press, 1992.

Gil, Juan. *Mitos y utopías del descubrimiento*. Madrid: Alianza Editorial, 1989.

Guillemard, F. H. H. *The Life of Ferdinand Magellan*. London: George Philip & Son, 1890.

Haliczer, Stephen. "The Expulsion of the Jews as Social Process." In *The Jews of Spain and the Expulsion of 1492*, ed. Moshe Lazar and Stephen Haliczer. Lancaster, CA: Labyrinthos, 1997.

Haring, Clarence Henry. *The Spanish Empire in America*. New York: Harcourt Brace & World, 1973. (Originally published in 1947.)

————. *Trade and Navigation Between Spain and the Indies*. Cambridge: Harvard University Press, 1918.

Harvey, Miles. *The Island of Lost Maps*. New York: Random House, 2000.

Hawthorne, Daniel. *Ferdinand Magellan*. Garden City, NY: Doubleday, 1964.

Henisch, Bridget Ann. *Fast and Feast*. University Park: Pennsylvania State University Press, 1976.

Herrera y Tordesillas, Antonio de. *The General History of the Vast Continent and Islands of America*, vols. 2 and 3. London: Jer. Batley, 1725. (Originally published in 1601–15.)

————. *Historia general de los hechos de los Castellanos en las islas i tierra firme del mar océano*, vol. 5. Madrid: Tipografía de Archivos, 1936.

Hewitt, John. *Ancient Armour and Weapons in Europe*, vol. 3. Graz, Austria: Akademische Druck, 1967.

Hildebrand, Arthur Sturges. *Magellan*. New York: Harcourt, Brace and Company, 1924.

Joyner, Tim. *Magellan*. Camden, ME: International Marine, 1992.

Kimble, George H. T. *Geography in the Middle Ages*. London: Methuen, 1938.

Lagôa, João António de Mascarenhas Judice, Visconde de. *Fernão de Magalhãis: a sua vida e a sua viagem*. 2 vols. Lisboa: Seara Nova, 1938.

Lalaguna, Juan. *A Traveller's History of Spain*, 4th ed. Brooklyn, NY, and Northampton, MA: Interlink Books, 1999.

Larner, John. *Marco Polo and the Discovery of the World*. New Haven: Yale University Press, 1999.

Leonardo de Argensola, Bartolomé. *Conquista de las islas Malucas*. Madrid: A. Martin, 1609.

———. *The Discovery and Conquest of the Molucco and Philippine Islands*, tr. John Stevens. London, 1708.

Levathes, Louise. *When China Ruled the Seas*. New York: Oxford University Press, 1996.

Lévesque, Rodrigue, ed. *History of Micronesia*, vol. 1. Gatineau, Québec: Lévesque Publications, n.d.

Licuanan, Virginia Benitz, and José Llavador Mira, eds. *The Philippines under Spain: A Compilation and Translation of Original Documents*, book 1. Manila: National Trust for Historical and Cultural Preservation of the Philippines, 1990.

Limborch, Philippus van. *The History of the Inquisition*, tr. Samuel Chandler. 2 vols. London: J. Gray, 1731.

López de Gómara, Francisco. *Historia general de las Indias*. Madrid: Amigos del Círculo del Bibliófilo, 1982.

Lothrop, Samuel Kirkland. *The Indians of Tierra del Fuego*. New York: Museum of the American Indian, 1928.

Lowes, John Livingston. *The Road to Xanadu*. Boston: Houghton Mifflin, 1927.

Macksey, Kenneth. *The Penguin Encyclopedia of Weapons and Military Technology*. London: Viking, 1993.

Manchester, William. *A World Lit Only by Fire: The Medieval Mind and the Renaissance*. New York: Little, Brown, 1993.

Markham, Clements, tr. *Early Spanish Voyages to the Strait of Magellan*. London: Hakluyt Society, 1911.

———, tr. *The Letters of Amerigo Vespucci*. London: Hakluyt Society, 1894.

Martinic Beros, Mateo. *Historia del Estrecho de Magallanes*. Santiago de Chile: Editorial Andrés Bello, 1977.

Medina, José Toribio, ed. *Colección de documentos inéditos para la historia de Chile*, vols. 2 and 3. Santiago de Chile: Imprenta Ercilla, 1888.

—————. *Colección de Historiadores de Chile y de Documentos Relativos*, vol. 27. Santiago de Chile: Imprenta Elzeviriana, 1901.

—————. *El descubrimiento del Océano Pacífico: Vasco Nuñez Balboa, Hernando de Magallanes y sus compañeros*. Santiago de Chile: Imprenta Elzeviriana, 1920.

Medina, Pedro de. *A Navigator's Universe*, tr. Ursula Lamb, Chicago: University of Chicago Press, 1972. (Originally published 1538.)

Melón y Ruiz de Gordejuela, Amando. *Magallanes-Elcano; o, La primera vuelta al mundo*. Zaragoza: Ediciones Luz, 1940.

Menzies, Gavin. *1421: The Year China Discovered America*. London: Bantam Press, 2002.

Merriman, Roger Bigelow. *The Rise of the Spanish Empire in the Old World and the New*. New York: Macmillan, 1925.

Milton, Giles. *Nathaniel's Nutmeg*. New York: Farrar, Straus and Giroux, 1999.

Mitchell, Mairin. *Elcano: The First Circumnavigator*. London: Herder Publications, 1958.

Mocatta, Frederic David. *The Jews of Spain and Portugal and the Inquisition*. New York: Cooper Square Publishers, 1973. (Originally published in 1933.)

Molina, Antonio de. *Historia de Filipinas*. 2 vols. Madrid: Ediciones Cultura Hispánica del Instituto de Cooperación Iberoamericana, 1984.

Morga, Antonio de. *Sucesos de las Islas Filipinas*, tr. J. S. Cummins. Cambridge: Hakluyt Society, 1971.

Morris, John G. *Martin Behaim*. Baltimore: Maryland Historical Society, 1855.

Morison, Samuel Eliot. *Admiral of the Ocean Sea*. 2 vols. Boston: Little, Brown, 1942.

————. *The European Discovery of America: The Northern Voyages.* New York: Oxford University Press, 1971.

————. *The European Discovery of America: The Southern Voyages.* New York: Oxford University Press, 1974.

Navarette, Martín Fernández de. *Colección de los viajes y descubrimientos que hicieron por mar los españoles desde fines del siglo XV.* 5 vols. Madrid: Imprenta Nacional, 1837.

Nimmo, Harry. *The Sea People of Sulu.* San Francisco: Chandler, 1972.

Nowell, Charles E., ed. *Magellan's Voyage Around the World.* Evanston, IL: Northwestern University Press, 1962.

Nunn, George E. *The Columbus and Magellan Concepts of South American Geography.* Glenside, 1932. (Privately printed.)

Obregón, Mauricio. *From Argonauts to Astronauts: An Unconventional History of Discovery.* New York: Harper & Row, 1980.

————. *La primera vuelta al mundo.* Bogotá: Plaza y Janés, 1984.

Oviedo y Valdez, Gonzalo Fernández de. *Historia general y natural de las Indias.* Asunción: Editorial Guaranía, 1944–45.

The Oxford Companion to Ships & the Sea, ed. Peter Kemp. London: Oxford University Press, 1976.

Parr, Charles McKew. *So Noble a Captain.* New York: Thomas Y. Crowell, 1953.

Parry, J. H. *The Age of Reconnaissance.* Berkeley: University of California Press, 1963.

————. *The Discovery of South America.* New York: Taplinger, 1979.

————. *The Discovery of the Sea.* Berkeley: University of California Press, 1981.

————. *The European Reconnaissance: Selected Documents.* New York: Walker and Co., 1968.

————. *The Spanish Seaborne Empire.* New York: Knopf, 1970.

Parry, John W. *The Story of Spices.* New York: Chemical Publishing Company, 1953.

Pearson, M. N., ed. *Spices in the Indian Ocean World.* Aldershot, Hampshire: Variorum, 1996.

Peillard, Leonce. *Magallanes.* Barcelona: Círculo de Lectores, 1970.

Penrose, Boies. A *Link to Magellan: Being a Chart of the East Indies, c. 1522*. Privately printed, 1929.

———. *Travel and Discovery in the Renaissance*. Cambridge: Harvard University Press, 1955.

Pérez-Mallaína, Pablo E. *Spain's Men of the Sea*, tr. Carla Rahn Phillips. Baltimore: Johns Hopkins University Press, 1998.

Pfitzer, Gregory M. *Samuel Eliot Morison's Historical World*. Boston: Northeastern University Press, 1991.

Pigafetta, Antonio. *Magellan's Voyage Around the World*, tr. James Alexander Robinson. 3 vols. Cleveland: Arthur H. Clark, 1906.

———. *Magellan's Voyage: A Narrative Account of the First Circumnavigation*, tr. R. A. Skelton. 2 vols. New Haven and London: Yale University Press, 1969.

———. *The Voyage of Magellan*, tr. Paula Spurlin Paige. Englewood Cliffs, NJ: Prentice-Hall, 1969.

Pike, Ruth. *Linajudos and Conversos in Seville*. New York: Peter Lang, 2000.

Polo, Marco. *The Travels*, tr. Ronald Latham. London: Penguin Books, 1958. (Originally written c. 1298.)

Prestage, Edgar. *The Portuguese Pioneers*. London: Adam and Charles Black, 1966. (Originally published in 1933.)

Ravenstein, E. G. *Martin Behaim: His Life and His Globe*. London: George Philip & Son, 1908.

Reau, Louis. *Iconographie de l'Art Chretien*. 3 vols. Paris: Presses Universitaires de France, 1955–59.

Reyes y Florentino, Isabelo de los. *Las islas Visayas en la época de la conquista*. Manila: Tipo-Litografía de Chofré, 1889.

Riling, Ray. *The Powder Flask Book*. New Hope, Pennsylvania: Robert Halter, 1953.

Roditi, Edouard. *Magellan of the Pacific*. London: Faber and Faber, 1972.

Rodríguez, Marco, and María del Rosario. *Catálogo de armas de fuego*. Madrid: Patronato Nacional de Museos, 1980.

Rogers, Robert F. *Destiny's Landfall: A History of Guam*. Honolulu: University of Hawaii Press, 1995.

Rosengarten, Frederic, Jr. *The Book of Spices*, rev. ed. New York: Pyramid Books, 1973.

Sagarra Gamazo, Adelaida. *La otra versión de la historia indiana: Colón y Fonseca.* Valladolid: Universidad de Valladolid, 1997.

Schivelbusch, Wolfgang. *Tastes of Paradise.* New York: Vintage Books, 1992.

Silverberg, Robert. *The Realm of Prester John.* Athens: Ohio University Press, 1996.

Sharp, Andrew. *The Discovery of the Pacific Islands.* London: Oxford University Press, 1960.

Shirley, Rodney. *The Mapping of the World: Early Printed World Maps, 1472–1700*, rev. ed. London: New Holland Press, 1993.

Slocum, Joshua. *Sailing Alone Around the World.* New York: Barnes & Noble Books, 2000.

Sobel, Dava. *Longitude.* New York: Penguin Books, 1996.

Stanley, Henry E. J. [Lord Stanley of Alderley], ed. *The First Voyage Round the World, by Magellan.* London: Hakluyt Society, 1874. (Reprinted 1964.)

The Travels of Sir John Mandeville, tr. C. W. R. D. Moseley. London: Penguin Books, 1983. (Originally written c. 1356–57.)

Torres y Lanzas, Pedro. *Catálogo de los documentos relativos a las islas Filipinas existentes en el Archivo de Indias de Sevilla*, vol. 1. Barcelona: L. Tasso, 1925.

Ulman, R. B., and D. Brothers. *The Shattered Self: A Psychoanalytic Study of Trauma.* Hillsdale, NJ: Analytic Press, 1988.

Vial, Ignacio Fernández, and Guadalupe Fernández Morente. *La primera vuelta al mundo: La nao Victoria.* Sevilla: Muñoz Moya Editores, 2001.

Vigón, Jorge, *Historia de la artillería Española.* Madrid, 1947.

Villas-Boas, Manuel. *Os Magalhães: sete séculos de aventura.* Lisboa: Estampa, 1998.

Wilford, John Noble. *The Mapmakers*, rev. ed. New York: Knopf, 2000.

Winsor, Justin. *Narrative and Critical History of America*, vol. 2. Boston: Houghton Mifflin, 1884.

Zweig, Stefan. *Conqueror of the Seas.* New York: Viking, 1938.

Periodicals

Laurioux, Bruno. "Spices in the Medieval Diet: A New Approach." *Food and Foodways*, 1, no. 1 (1985).

Nunn, George E. "Magellan's Route in the Pacific." *Geographical Review* 24 (1934).

Pike, Ruth. "Seville in the Sixteenth Century." *Hispanic American Historical Review* 41, no. 3 (August 1961).

Rogers, Robert F., and Dirk Anthony Ballendorf. "Magellan's Landfall in the Mariana Islands." *Journal of Pacific History* 24 (October 1989).

Taylor, Paul S. "Spanish Seamen in the New World during the Colonial Period." *Hispanic American Historical Review* 5 (1922).

Torodash, Martin. "Magellan Historiography." *Hispanic American Historical Review* 51, no. 2 (May 1971).

Villiers, Alan. "Magellan: A Voyage into the Unknown Changed Man's Understanding of His World." *National Geographic*, June 1976.

Winchester, Simon. "After Dire Straits, an Agonizing Haul Across the Pacific." *Smithsonian*, April 1991, pp. 84–95.

Wroth, Lawrence C. "The Early Cartography of the Pacific." *Papers of the Bibliographical Society of America* 38. New York: Bibliographical Society of America, 1944.

Unpublished Materials

Gallego, Vasquito. "The Voyage of Fernão de Magalhães Written by One Man Who Went in His Company," tr. Samuel Eliot Morison. Harvard University Archives.

Morison, Samuel Eliot. Unpublished article for *Life*, February 24, 1972. Harvard University Archives.

Sandman, Alison. *Cosmographers vs. Pilots: Navigation, Cosmography, and the State in Early Modern Spain*, PhD dissertation. University of Wisconsin, 2001.

Smith, Roger Craig. *Vanguard of Empire: 15th- and 16th-century Iberian Ship Technology in the Age of Discovery.* PhD dissertation. Texas A&M University, 1989.

Special Collections Department, Brandeis University Libraries. Documents pertaining to lawsuits over the outcome of Magellan's voyage.

INDEX

211